SEVEN
Andrew Kevin Walker

ff

faber and faber

First published in 1999
by Faber and Faber Limited
3 Queen Square London WC1N 3AU
This edition published in 2000

Photoset by Parker Typesetting Service, Leicester
Printed in England by Mackays of Chatham plc, Chatham, Kent

A CIP record for this book
is available from the British Library

ISBN 0–571–20284–5

2 4 6 8 10 9 7 5 3 1

CONTENTS

INTRODUCTION

Seeing *Seven* for the first time left me reeling. As I sat wedged in a
London preview screening between two terrified women – one of
whom hated horror films and who literally couldn't bear to watch
– *Seven* seemed less a movie than an insidious assault on the mind
and the senses. I felt abused by images at once beautiful and
disturbing, baroque and apocalyptic, by a story that dared pull
back the veil of contemporary Hollywood movie normality to
reveal a world of such overwhelming desperation and pessimism,
such depravity, horror and sickness that it stirred one's soul and
gnawed at the gut. From its haunting opening title sequence
through to its grim, uncompromising, truly shocking climax which
so ruthlessly and effectively pilloried Hollywood's tendency
towards artificially upbeat, happy endings, scarcely had a movie
affected me so profoundly.

Later I interviewed the film's director, David Fincher, for
Empire and met its writer Andrew Kevin Walker at an awards
ceremony in London where he picked up the award for Best Film
for *Seven*. Since then Walker and I have remained in contact.

Walker was born in 1964 in fabulously named Altoona,
Pennsylvania, and after high school studied film at Penn State
University. Having graduated, and faced with the decision of
moving to either New York or Los Angeles to pursue a career in
screenwriting, he opted for New York mainly, he says, because he
couldn't afford a car. He found work as a production assistant or
in the art department for various ultra low-budget movies,
including *Robot Holocaust*, before deciding he needed a forty-hour-
a-week job which would enable him to focus on his writing.

Walker spent three years working at Tower Records on
Broadway and 66th Street, and it was while he was employed there
that he wrote the script for *Seven*, which eventually helped him
secure an agent. The script took three months to sell, and after it
was optioned he moved to LA to pursue writing full-time.
Although it was almost five years before *Seven* was finally released
in 1995, the script served Walker well enough as a writing sample

to secure other screenwriting work, including the Marvel comic book adaptation *X Men*, as well as an adaptation of Dean R. Koonz's novel, *Hideaway*, which, despite Walker retaining a co-writing credit on the film, contains barely six words of his and only one or two scenes. In the meantime, an earlier Walker script for another low-budget horror film called *Brainscan* – again written while he was at Tower – was produced, though the first Walker knew of it was when it hit US cinemas. *Seven* had initially been purchased by an Italian production company for Jeremiah Chechik to direct, but when Chechik went off to make *Benny & Joon* the project found its way over to producer Arnold Kopelson and New Line, the Hollywood studio responsible for the *A Nightmare on Elm Street* series. Directed by David Fincher, whose sole feature credit then was the third part of the *Alien* saga, and starring Morgan Freeman and Brad Pitt, *Seven* was released in September 1995 and on its initial release made more than $100 million at the US box office. Walker himself appears as the victim of a shooting in the film's opening minutes.

In the five years since *Seven's* release, Walker has written a number of screenplays including an adaptation of Somerset Maugham's *Of Human Bondage* for Turner Pictures (Morgan Freeman's character in *Seven* was named after its author, a favourite of Walker) and *Red, White, Black and Blue* for Oliver Stone's Illusion Entertainment, a script which he calls 'a rip-off/ homage to every seventies cop movie ever made, in the vein of *Freebie and the Bean*', and which Walter Hill was at one point due to direct. He also wrote teleplays for HBO's *Tales from the Crypt* and *Perversions of Science*, as well as working as a script doctor, contributing production polishes to David Fincher's *The Game* and *Fight Club*. Another Walker screenplay, an adaptation of Washington Irving's 'The Legend of Sleepy Hollow', entitled *Sleepy Hollow*, went into production in England in late 1998, directed by Tim Burton and starring Johnny Depp, Christina Ricci and Miranda Richardson. The following interview took place shortly after the US release of *8mm* in March 1999.

Mark Salisbury

MARK SALISBURY: *Most aspiring screenwriters point to getting an agent as the toughest hurdle in selling their work. Do you agree?*
ANDREW KEVIN WALKER: It's a huge hurdle, one of many. It's a real catch-22 because agents and production companies won't look at material unless you've been produced, and how can you get produced unless you have an agent? It's one of those by-hook-or-by-crook situations. If you know *anybody* who works in the entertainment industry – and almost everybody knows *somebody*, whether it's the brother-in-law of an uncle of an actor or producer or director – you really have to exhaust all possible favours from friends and friends of friends' friends, trying to find someone to read your writing.

How did you manage to find an agent then?
I'm afraid to tell, because I don't want to invite people to start sending their scripts to me or to David Koepp. Nine years ago, I saw *Bad Influence*, a film David wrote, and I called him up, spoke to his assistant and said I'm writing a script and since agents won't look at anything unless it's recommended by someone they know, would David read it, and if he likes it, will he show it to his agent? David happened to be the nicest guy in the world and called me back the next day. I finished *Seven* as quickly as I could, sent it to him and he showed it to his agent, Gavin Polone. I remember the day Gavin called me in my tiny New York apartment and said he would represent the script. I literally leapt for joy. I was still working at Tower Records while he sent the script out. It went to many of the major studios. When a spec script makes the rounds, you're hoping it's going to sell for a million dollars but you're not surprised when all the studios come back and say they're not interested, which was the case with *Seven*. It went to a second bunch of studios and production companies, and they all passed, too. Eventually Jeremiah Chechik was interested enough that an Italian company, Penta Films, optioned the script for him. And, speaking of agents, I have to mention the *enormous* debt I owe Missy Malkin, who was also my agent, and the greatest friend anyone could ever ask for.

Getting an agent is a matter of being an annoyance, but an important aspect of being an annoyance – and I stress this, being a person at this point who could be annoyed – is that if you ask someone to read your script and they can't, then you've got to move on to the next possibility. I've had people ask me to read their scripts, and if I'm able to time-wise, I'll do it, but if I can't, I only want to have to say no maybe twice. I've actually had a guy with a script show up in my apartment building looking for me, which was harmless, but still creeped me out.

When you begin writing a script, do you have everything worked out in advance or do you let the story flow organically?
I hate everything I write actually, so I doubt if my advice has much worth. I have to know almost everything structurally and narratively before I start, especially on assignments, since I'm worried nothing will flow and then I'll have to give back the money. Three act structure was drilled into me by my screenwriting professor Jeff Rush at Penn State. I read every book I could find about screenwriting, which I recommend because you retain what you believe in and discard the rest. I found Syd Field's *Screenplay* a good, basic textbook. Three act structure is the key, without trying to get too paint-by-numbers. I need to know the end of the first act, approximate mid-point and end of the second act, and I think you must know your ending. Hook the reader in the first ten pages, or that might be all they read – that kind of thing.

I try to know my main character's conflict. That's the cliché, and it's true. Conflict is story, story is conflict, in every character, every scene, every line of dialogue, hopefully. Conflict informs the structure. I write down my character's name and draw two arrows on either side, arrows pulling in opposite directions. For *Seven*, Somerset is pulled in one direction by KEEP FIGHTING and in the other direction by GIVE UP. That's what he's about, wanting to quit, desiring apathy and escape, and at the same time not being able to avoid caring. In the end, your character makes their choice, one way or the other, or they stay in the middle. It may be that there is no 'character arc', which is great, but hard to get away with sometimes.

I outline. I have to see the entire script on one page, a page divided into three columns, with a very brief description of every single scene. That way I can see if the act balance feels right. Of course, everything can change once you start typing. Writing *8mm*, I thought all along that the third act was going to be about the private investigator, Welles, tracking down and killing three other characters. But, near the end of the second act, I realized it would be too long and too repetitive. I was sitting at the computer screen, and there was a gun pointed at one character, Dino Velvet, and I thought, 'Wouldn't it be great if the gun went off?' So, the gun went off.

This is all pretty obvious, I suppose. After a long, healthy period of fear-filled procrastination, I start writing. I try to build in subtext. Since scripts are all about action and dialogue, since you're not inside characters' heads as in novels, underlying subtext is huge. Characters should say one thing and mean another. The trick is to try to write scenes so that the audience understands what each character truly means, truly wants, in spite of what your characters say to each other. I often fail at that.

Do you think screenwriters can learn from reading other people's scripts?
It is important to read other scripts, even just to see how things are laid out on the page. You know, until you sit down to write a script you don't realize what a complex puzzle it is you're trying to solve; how voice-over plays in certain scenes, how to keep phone conversations from being expositionally boring, how easy it is to get bogged down in the second act, how much room there is to describe any given scene. I overwrite, so that's a problem. You should be economical. You might want to use three paragraphs to describe a room, or you may feel you need half a page to describe what a character looks like, what they wear, what cigarettes they smoke. But, if you're concise with your prose and you're able to win the readers over into your story even in the smallest way, the readers will take your brief descriptions and imagine the best version of the scenes, the characters and the settings for themselves. That's the balance I was taught to try to strike, making your story 'fully imagined' without overwriting.

The idea behind Seven *is, fundamentally, a very exploitational one. Where did the concept come from?*
I was working at Tower Records and writing for a small production company [working] on movies like *Brainscan* and *Bloodrush*, there was even something they wanted to do called *Abusement Park*. My mind was in an exploitational vein. It also had a lot to do with living in New York City and how depressed I was

living there. I'm from suburban Pennsylvania, with backyards and grass and birds and trees. New York was quite a culture shock for me.

Did you witness any violence first-hand or was it the atmosphere of the city that fed into the script?
I've said many times that *Seven* was my love letter to New York City. I saw plenty of troubling things. In any big city, you see things every day that if you dwell on them you're going to be miserable. If you walk down the street and pass a homeless person begging for money, whether you give them money or not, two blocks later there'll be another homeless person. Five blocks later, if you're still dwelling on the inherent tragedy of what you've seen, you'll be unable to function. There's a required apathy in big cities, in life in general – you have to carry enough apathy to make it through the day, unfortunately. If you walk out your front door and the street's strewn with trash, and there's a car that's been abandoned, and a week later that car's still there, but the windows are smashed in, and a week after that the car's still there, but it's burnt out – if that's the environment you live in, why not throw your own garbage into the street? Apathy breeds apathy.

The film presents three very distinct viewpoints to that problem. There's Somerset who's resigned to the apathy and wants to give up on it. Mills who feels, rather naively, that he can make a difference and save the world, and John Doe who's out to change the world but in a different way.
That movie, while exploitational, hopefully became a little bit more than that. A good example may be the metronome that Somerset uses to fall asleep. He focuses on that metronome's ticking so he's able to shut out the noise of the city, the car horns and the voices that come through the walls. That came from a personal place – you hear sirens all night and people yelling and screaming at each other from across the street. Somerset survives by focusing; in the same way he attempts to concentrate on the small details of a murder he's trying to solve, rather than focusing on the bigger picture where all the tragedy and sadness exists.

Somerset is fed up. He's a character who desperately needs apathy, because he's spent so many years without a capacity to be apathetic. His character comes from a place in me, being sad, feeling put upon by the place I was living in. I had to say to myself, if you're so trodden down by this environment, what are your choices? You can either walk away, quit or cower – which I'm good at by the way, I cower well – or you can keep going. Somerset wants to give up. All the arguments he has with Mills about the fact that they're never going to make a difference, well . . . I don't think Somerset realizes the only thing worse than having everyone tell him he's wrong, is having someone tell him he's right. When Somerset's pessimism is confirmed in the end, I don't think he wants to accept it.

There's more Somerset in me than Mills' belief that he can go out there and make a difference. Although Somerset is intelligent, and I'd be digging out the *Cliff Notes* like Mills. Mills' character is each of our best, sometimes misguided, intentions. John Doe is fairly obvious, being everyone's worst kind of secret desires and wishes, taken to the extreme. John Doe is a guy who walks down the street and can't stop thinking about the tragedy and squalor and immorality and injustice, and it all builds up in him. He doesn't have an apathy defense mechanism. His line about how you can see one of the seven deadly sins on every street corner and in every home, well that's true of New York City. That's part of where his character came from.

One of the things that makes the film so powerful is that while John Doe's methods obviously cannot be justified, you can at least sympathize with his point of view.
The hope was that all three characters make arguments that, on some level, you can agree with. Although you may be loath to admit it, you've felt some of the frustration John Doe feels, some of the things he espouses in that car ride in the third act. It's a great credit to David Fincher. When he and I sat down over the rewrite of *Seven*, David wanted to make sure there was at least something in each of those three voices that you could agree with. He stressed that.

You mentioned David Fincher, whom you've credited for Seven's *success and with whom you've since worked on* The Game *and* Fight Club. *Can you describe your relationship with him?*
Because I was incredibly lucky with *Seven* – so pleased with the movie and with how it exceeded my expectations – let's just say

I'm relearning how inherently unsatisfying the career of a screenwriter can be. I'm very glad to be doing what I'm doing, and grateful and undeserving, but *8mm*, at a certain point in the process, became something other than happy. Even *Sleepy Hollow*, which I worked on for a very long time, got rewritten by Tom Stoppard just before it went into production – and if you're going to be rewritten by anybody, Tom Stoppard's the guy, it's an honor – but regardless of whether it became a better or worse script, it wasn't as much *my* script. That's the thing. Being rewritten comes with the territory, and so be it, but it's wearying. Often, the only time anything you write is going to be what you intend it to be is the moment you finish it. That's just the way it is.

When you become part of the collaborative process, the very best you can hope for is that you'll be in agreement with the director, that you'll be of like mind. It's great when the ideas he or she brings to the process make sense to you and you implement them gladly. With *Seven*, that was absolutely the case. I don't know why, but Fincher and I have been of a like mind. I trust him implicitly. I know my voice is heard when he's overseeing a rewrite, and I know my opinions count for something, and I really appreciate that. Fincher read the first draft of *Seven*, with the head in the box ending, and he called up his agent and said, 'God, are they really going to make this?' His agent said, I believe, 'Oh, head in the box, you've got the wrong draft.' Fincher was sent the draft I had rewritten for Jeremiah Chechik – it had more stereotypically creepy suspense and a completely different ending, a big set-piece ending in a burnt-out church – and Fincher wanted to go back to the first draft. That's a very specific example of how David Fincher came along and fought for the thing I had been fighting for all along and, in my opinion, he saved the movie completely.

Didn't Brad Pitt also have it written in his contract that they couldn't change the ending?

I think so. New Line is a great place for movies that are a little off the beaten track, but even New Line and Kopelson were wary of the original ending, and they wanted to change it. It would have been changed if David and Brad and Morgan and Kevin Spacey hadn't fought to keep it the way it is now.

Seven constantly confounds expectations. You think initially it's a buddy movie, then it turns into a serial killer movie, then it becomes something else entirely, namely a meditation on the nature of evil. And throughout, the film eschews the conventions of the cop genre, like having John Doe turn up outside his apartment when the cops knock at his door or give himself up to the police.

With *Seven* I didn't know the whole story when I started, since I was only writing it for myself. I structured it loosely, knew where the murders would fall and what murder would represent each sin. I wanted to spend time trudging along with the police, without having the story jump omnipotently to see what the villain was up to in the meantime. Having John Doe abruptly show up to take shots at them seemed a good way to have their paths cross, suddenly and violently. I also knew all along that John Doe would turn himself in at the end of the second act. I wanted John Doe captured in the most unsatisfying way possible, so it would be frustrating and devoid of any sense of accomplishment, to keep the story off balance.

Didn't the ending, even once it was decided to keep the head in the box, go through a number of revisions?

There was a draft done for New Line which had Somerset shooting John Doe, because at least that meant John Doe didn't win completely. I always thought John Doe needed to win completely. Then there was a draft where Brad's character shoots John Doe, and the movie goes immediately to black. Credits roll. That was what Fincher liked, and that was fine by me since anyone watching could interpret it however they wanted. The ending that got shot and used was the compromise made to please New Line, and I was fine with that too, since in the first draft it was strongly implied that Somerset ends up staying in the city. As is, I believe Somerset's last line in the film is, 'Around. I'll be around.'

PUBLISHER'S NOTE

The draft of *Seven* featured is the third draft, dated 3 October 1994 which was fairly close to the end of the rewrite process – 85–90 per cent, says Walker – and incorporates notes from David Fincher, Brad Pitt, producer Arnold Kopelson, as well as New Line.

A NOTE ABOUT THE FORMAT

For the purposes of publication, the layout of the script in this book bears little resemblance to true screenplay format. This information will be of interest only to film students and to those wishing to write scripts of their own – well, who else is going to be reading this anyway? There are many textbooks on screenwriting which address the specifics of format. *The Complete Guide to Standard Script Formats; Part I: The Screenplay* by Judith H. Haag and Hillis R. Cole, Jr., is a good one if you can find it. *Screenplay* by Syd Field has an entire chapter devoted to format, as does *The Elements of Screen-writing* by Irwin R. Blacker. There are computer software programs, such as *Scriptware* and *Final Draft*, which have formatting built in.

While all rules are made to be broken, without at least some semblance of proper script format your writing mey be unfairly dismissed as unprofessional. Same problem occurs when you write your entire script in crayon, so consider yourself warned. The rules of formatting, in part, create an approximate page-to-screen ratio of *one script page = one minute screen time*. Not surprisingly, many screenplays are around 120 pages in length, or about two hours. *Seven* was 129 pages, give or take. (Told you I overwrite.) With regard to three act structure, there are notations within the script to indicate what I consider the *end of the first act* and the *end of the second act*.

A. K. W.

Seven

Credits

INT. OLD HOUSE – DAY

Sunlight comes through the soot on the windows, more brown than bright. SOMERSET, 45, stands in one corner of this small, second-story room. He looks over the ceiling, looks down at the worn wooden floors, looks at the peeling wallpaper.

He walks to the center of the room, continues his study, taking his time. He halts, turns to one wall where the current wallpaper is torn away to reveal flowery wallpaper underneath.

Somerset goes to this wall and runs his finger across one of the pale, red roses which decorates the older paper. He pushes the grime away, brings the rose out more clearly.

He reaches into his suit pocket and takes out a switchblade. He flips the thin, lethal blade free. Working deliberately, delicately, Somerset cuts a square around the rose, then peels the square of dry wallpaper away from the wall. He studies it in his hand.

EXT. OLD HOUSE – DAY

Somerset stands in front of the old home. He looks out at the surrounding farms and forests. He ponders something. Birds sing.

MAN
(off-screen)

Is something wrong?

Somerset does not respond, just stares off. The MAN, 34, wears a real-estate broker's jacket and stands beside a FOR SALE *sign in the muddy lawn.*

Is there something the matter?

Somerset turns to face the Man, then looks back at the house.

SOMERSET

No. No . . . it's just that everything here seems . . . so strange.

MAN

Strange? There's nothing strange about this place. The house'll need a little fixing up, that's for sure . . .

SOMERSET

No. I like the house, and this place.

MAN

I was going to say. 'Cause this place is about as normal as places get.

Somerset nods, taking a deep breath. He smiles.

SOMERSET

That's what I mean.

Somerset looks back to the beautiful landscape. The man does not understand, just shakes his head as he pulls the FOR SALE sign out of the ground.

INT. AMTRAK TRAIN – LATER – DAY

Somerset is in the window seat, looking out of the window of the speeding train, smoking a cigarette. He is near the back of the car, away from the few other passengers.

Outside, farms, fields, small homes and lawns rush by. The panorama is dappled by the rays of the soon to be setting sun.

INT. AMTRAK TRAIN – LATER – DAY

The train is almost full, moving slower. Somerset has his suitcase on the aisle seat beside him. He holds a hardcover book unopened on his lap. He still stares out of the window, but his face is tense. The train is passing an ugly, swampy field. The sun has gone under.

Though it seems impossible that it could ever have got there, a car's burnt-out skeleton sits rusting in the bracken.

Ahead, the city waits. The sky is full of smokestacks and huge industrial cranes.

INT. AMTRAK TRAIN – LATER – DAY

The train is passing urban streets below. Slums and smashed cars. People stand on groups on the corners. Bleak.

Somerset's suitcase is now on the window seat. Somerset has moved to the aisle. He is reading his book. He looks up from the book and rubs his eyes, then looks back to continue reading, not once looking out the window.

EXT. CITY STREET – NIGHT

Somerset carries his suitcase outside the train station. The city demands attention: cars screeching, people yelling, sirens blaring.

Somerset passes a family of bewildered tourists. A WEIRD MAN has a hand on the tourist father's suitcase. It has become a tugging match with the Weird Man shouting, 'I'll take you to a taxi . . . I'll take you.' Ahead, a group is gathered on the sidewalk near two ambulances. People clamor to get a look at a BLOODY BODY which lies on the street.

Policemen try to hold the crowd off. Ambulance attendants administer aid to the victim, who convulses. Somerset moves by, ignoring it all. He motions for a cab. One pulls up from the street's stream of vehicles.

INT. CAB. – NIGHT

Somerset throws his suitcase in and shuts the door behind him.

> CAB DRIVER
> (*about the crowd*)
> What's the big fuss?

Somerset looks out at the crowd, looks at the driver.

> SOMERSET
> Do you care?

> CAB DRIVER
> (*under his breath*)
> Well, excuse me all to hell.

The Driver leans forward, checking it out. The circle of spectators shifts suddenly. A man has shoved another man and they're really going at it now. They swing at each other and tear at each other's clothing. One man's flailing fist connects and the other man's face is instantly bloodied. The fight grows even more frantic. Policemen try to stop it.

Crazy fucks.

The Driver pulls away and the cab rages down the street. Somerset watches the parade of neon passing on the avenue. He slumps back in the seat and closes his eyes.

Where you headed?

Somerset opens his eyes.

SOMERSET

Far away from here.

INT. SOMERSET'S APARTMENT – NIGHT

The curtains are closed. The SOUNDS of the CITY are here, as they will be everywhere in this story. A CAR ALARM is SOUNDING, shrill and clear. Somerset's life is packed into moving boxes, except for some clothing in a closet and hundreds and hundreds of books on the shelves of one wall. Somerset is lying on the bed, dressed only in his underwear.

He reaches to the nightstand, to a wooden, pyramidical metronome. He frees the metronome's weighted swing-arm so it moves back and forth. Swings to the left – TICK, swings to the right – TICK. Tick . . . tick . . . tick . . . measured and steady.

Somerset situates on the bed, closes his eyes. Tick . . . tick . . . tick. The metronome's sound competes with the sound of the car alarm. Somerset's face tightens as he concentrates on the metronome. His eyes close tighter. Tick . . . tick . . . tick. The swing-arm moves evenly. Somerset's breathing deepens.

Tick . . . tick . . . tick. The car alarm seems quieter.

Tick . . . tick . . . tick. Somerset continues his concentration. The metronome's sound seems louder.

Tick . . . tick . . . tick. The sound of the car alarm fades, and is GONE. The metronome is the only sound.

Somerset's face relaxes as he begins to fall asleep. Tick . . . tick . . . tick . . .

INSERT – TITLE CARD: SUNDAY

INT. SOMERSET'S APARTMENT – MORNING

Quiet. Somerset stands before a mirror, tying his tie. He does it carefully, making sure the knot is neat and tight, smoothing the collar and the front of his shirt.

Next, he takes his suit jacket off the neatly made bed. He holds the jacket up on its hanger, brushing off a speck and inspecting it before sliding it on.

Somerset picks items off a moving box: his keys, wallet, switchblade, gold Homicide badge. Finally, he opens the hardcover book he had with him on the train. From the pages, he takes the pale, paper rose.

INT. TENEMENT APARTMENT – DAY

Somerset stands before a wall which is stained by a star-burst of blood. A body lies on the floor under a sheet. A sawed-off shotgun lies not far from the body. The apartment is gloomy.

DETECTIVE TAYLOR, 52, stands on the other side of the room, looks through a notepad.

> TAYLOR
> Neighbors heard them screaming at each other for like two hours. It was nothing new. But, then they heard the gun go off. Both barrels.

> SOMERSET
> Did the wife confess?

> TAYLOR
> When the patrolmen came she was trying to put his head together. She was crying too hard to say anything.

Somerset begins walking around the apartment.

> SOMERSET
> Why always like this? Only after the fact . . . this sudden realization that person will cease to exist.

9

TAYLOR

Crime of passion.

SOMERSET

Yes. Look at all the passion on the wall here.

TAYLOR

This is a done deal. All but the paperwork.

Taylor shifts his weight, impatient. Somerset looks at a coloring book open on the coffee table. There are crayons beside it. Somerset picks the book up, flips through the pages.

SOMERSET

Did the son see it happen?

TAYLOR

I don't know.

Taylor closes his notebook, perturbed.

Somerset looks at the pictures of cute, crudely colored animals.

What kind of fucking question is that anyway?

Taylor walks over and grabs the coloring book to get his attention.

You know, we're all real glad we're getting rid of you, Somerset. You know that? I mean, it's always these questions with you . . . 'Did the kid see it?' Well, who gives a fuck? Huh?
                    (*points*)
He's dead. His wife killed him.

Taylor throws the coloring book back to Somerset and walks.

Anything else has nothing to do with us.

Taylor leaves, pushing past DETECTIVE DAVID MILLS, 31, who is just entering. Mills is muscular and handsome. He looks back at Taylor, then around the apartment, a bit disoriented.

Somerset puts down the coloring book. He stares at the floor, showing no reaction to Taylor's tantrum.

MILLS

Uh, Lieutenant Somerset?

Somerset looks to see Mills.

EXT. CITY STREET – DAY

A body bag is carried through a crowd of people outside the tenement building. Somerset follows the body bag out and Mills follows Somerset. They walk towards the end of the filthy block, past a man urinating on a car.

MILLS

I'm a little thrown. I just got in town like twenty minutes ago and they dumped me here.

SOMERSET

Since we're just starting out, Detective Mills, I thought we could go to a bar . . . sit and talk for a while. After that, we'll . . .

MILLS
(*interrupting*)

Actually, if it's all the same, I'd like to get to the precinct house asap. Seeing how we don't have much time for this whole transition thing.

Somerset keeps walking, says nothing.

I need to start getting the feel of it all, right? Meet the people.

SOMERSET

I meant to ask you something, when we spoke on the phone. I can't help wondering . . . Why here?

MILLS

I . . . I don't follow.

SOMERSET

With all this effort you've made to get transferred, it's the first question that pops into my head.

MILLS

I'm here for the same reasons as you, I guess. Or, at least, the

same reasons you used to have before . . . before you decided
to . . . quit.

Somerset stops and faces Mills.

> SOMERSET

You just met me.

> MILLS

Maybe I'm not understanding the question.

> SOMERSET

It's very simple. You fought to get reassigned as if your life
depended on it. I've just never seen it done that way before,
Detective.

> MILLS

I thought I could do more good here. I don't know. Look,
it'd be great by me if we didn't start right off kicking each
other in the balls. But, you're calling the shots, Lieutenant, so
. . . however you want it to go.

> SOMERSET

Let me tell you how I want this to go. I want you to look, and
I want you to listen.

> MILLS

I wasn't standing around guarding the local Taco Bell. I've
worked homicide for five and a half years.

> SOMERSET

Not here.

> MILLS

I realize that.

> SOMERSET

Well, over the next seven days, do me the favor of
remembering it.

*Somerset turns and walks away. Mills stands a moment, pissed. He
follows after Somerset.*

INSERT – TITLE CARD: MONDAY

INT. SOMERSET'S APARTMENT — EARLY MORNING

Somerset lies asleep in bed. It is still dark outside. The phone beside the inactive metronome RINGS. Somerset awakens suddenly, startled. He looks towards the phone.

INT. MILLS' APARTMENT. BEDROOM — EARLY MORNING

It is just becoming light outside. Mills is wide awake in bed beside the sleeping form of his wife, TRACY, 30. Mills looks tired. He listens to passing traffic. He covers his eyes with his forearm.

He takes his arm away and, frustrated, sits up on the edge of the bed. This gets the attention of TWO DOGS lying on the floor, a golden retriever and a collie, who look to Mills. The room is a shambles, filled with moving boxes.

Light coming through the window glows upon a football trophy sticking out from one box. Large and noble, a golden player stands in frozen motion at the trophy's pinnacle.

Mills looks at the trophy and a fond smile forms on his face. The PHONE RINGS. Mills looks towards it. Tracy awakens. She looks up with half-opened eyes, a beautiful woman.

> TRACY
>
> What is it?

Phone rings. Mills reaches to touch Tracy's shoulder.

> MILLS
>
> It's okay.

Mills leans to get the phone. Tracy seems frightened.

> TRACY
>
> Honey . . . where are we?

EXT. APARTMENT BUILDING. ALLEYWAY — EARLY MORNING

Somerset and Mills, both wearing badges, walk with OFFICER DAVIS, a beefy, uniformed cop. They pass police cars and head into a trash-strewn alleyway. Davis hands Somerset two flashlights.

DAVIS

Everything's like I found it. I didn't touch anything.

SOMERSET

What time did you confirm the death?

DAVIS

Like I said, I didn't touch him, but he's had his face in a plate of spaghetti for about forty-five minutes now.

They reach a rusty side door, which Davis pulls open.

INT. APARTMENT BUILDING. STAIRWELL – EARLY MORNING

They enter a dark, ugly stairwell.

MILLS
(*to Davis*)

Hold on . . . you mean you didn't check for vital signs?

DAVIS

Did I stutter? Believe me, he ain't breathing, unless he's breathing spaghetti sauce.

MILLS

The point is . . .

DAVIS

Begging your pardon, but the guy's sitting in a pile of his own shit. If he ain't dead, he would've stood up by now.

Mills is angry, about to speak, but Somerset heads him off.

SOMERSET
(*to Davis*)

Thank you, officer. We'll need to talk to you again, after we've looked around.

DAVIS

Yes, sir.

Davis walks out, eyeing Mills. Mills watches him go. The rusty door slams shut behind Davis. It's very dark. Somerset turns on his flashlight, hands the other to Mills and starts upstairs.

SOMERSET

I wonder what exactly was the point of the conversation you were about to get into?

MILLS

And I wonder how many times he's found bodies that weren't really dead until he was in the car calling it in and eating a donut.

SOMERSET

Drop it.

MILLS

For now.

INT. APARTMENT BUILDING. HALLWAY – EARLY MORNING

Somerset comes from the stairwell, looking down the dank hall. At the end of the hall, a door is open. The light of a CAMERA FLASH spills out from that room every few seconds.

Mills and Somerset move on. Somerset takes out rubber gloves and slips them on, looking at something on the floor ahead. A yellow RECYCLING BIN sits just outside the door. It contains many neat, string-bound stacks of issues of READER'S DIGEST.

INT. APARTMENT. LIVING-ROOM – EARLY MORNING

There are lights on in this room. Lamps with dusty shades. A few porn mags on a table. Somerset and Mills cross.

A couch against one wall is piled with yellowed, once-white pillows. It faces two small televisions, both on with no sound.

INT. APARTMENT. KITCHEN – EARLY MORNING

Somerset and Mills enter, using their flashlights in the dark. Mills takes out a handkerchief, covering his nose. ERIC is crouched on the floor, putting camera equipment away. He's wearing a medical mask over his face. He hoists his bag and moves past the detectives.

ERIC

Enjoy.

Eric leaves. Somerset sweeps the room with his flashlight . . .

At the stove, each burner has a used pot or pan on it. Food has been slopped there and on the adjoining counter-top and sink. Used utensils are everywhere, along with empty tin cans and jars. Cockroaches swarm.

The flashlight beam follows a trail of dripped sauces, soups and crumbs of food across the floor from the stove to a kitchen table. The kitchen table is covered in soiled paper plates which hold bits of half-eaten sandwiches, potatoes, beef stew, donuts and many other junk foods.

The kitchen is tiny; barely enough room for three people. The kitchen table is at the center of the room. An OBESE MAN is slumped forward in a kitchen chair. He is face down, dead in a plate of spaghetti.

> MILLS
>
> Jeez . . . somebody phone Guinness. I think we've got a record here.

Mills walks to the dead man, leaning to study, without touching.

> Who said this was murder?

> SOMERSET
>
> No one yet.

> MILLS
>
> Are we wasting our time? This guy's heart's got to be the size of a canned ham. If this isn't a coronary, I don't know what is.

Somerset moves his flashlight beam down the obese corpse, stops at the man's feet. Somerset kneels.

At the obese man's pants cuff, there's a tiny point of metal sticking out. Somerset uses a pen to lift the pants leg. Razor wire is tied around the swollen, purple ankle.

> Or not.

Somerset stands and steps back. Mills bends to take his place, looking under the table and shining his flashlight into the corpse's lap. The obese man's bloated hands are folded there, bound tightly with rope.

16

He might have tied himself up . . . make it look like murder. I
saw a guy once, wanted his family to collect life insurance, right?

*Somerset does not listen. He is focused on the corpse, studies the back of
the man's head and neck. He runs his pen against the back of the
corpse's neck, combing the hair upwards.*

*There are small circular and semi-circular BRUISES on the back of the
obese man's head and neck, some hidden under the hair.*

We found him . . . knife in his back. Except, I finally figured
out . . . he held the knife behind him . . . put the tip of it
between his shoulder-blades, got real close to the wall and
grabbed on to the door jamb . . .

SOMERSET
(*irritated*)
Please be quiet for a while, would you?

*Mills looks up at Somerset from below. Somerset remains focused on the
bruises.*

MILLS
(*sarcastic*)
Forgive me.

*Mills stands and walks around to the other side of the table, where he
gets down again.*

There's something here.

SOMERSET
What?

MILLS
There's a bucket. Under the table.

*Somerset crouches, pulls up the cheap tablecloth on his side of the table.
A METAL BUCKET sits under the table.*

SOMERSET
What is it?

*Mills slides under with his flashlight, angling in the confined space to
look. He is repulsed and pulls back.*

MILLS

It's vomit.

Mills stands and backs away, near the refrigerator, not wanting to be anywhere near the bucket.

It's a bucket of vomit.

SOMERSET

Is there any blood in it?

MILLS

I don't know. Feel free to look for yourself, okay?

Somerset stands, stares at the obese man. He shakes his head, perplexed. There is a KNOCK at the door. The detectives look to see DOCTOR THOMAS O'NEILL, 52, the medical examiner, in the doorway. O'Neill is looking at the ceiling. He flicks the light switch. No light, so he flicks the switch up and down.

O'NEILL

Wonderful.

O'Neill seems a bit gone. He drops his black bag on to the floor beside the corpse. He begins to sort through the bag, surgical tools clinking together.

Mills turns to open the refrigerator. It's nearly empty.

MILLS
(*to Somerset*)

You think it was poison?

SOMERSET

Guessing is useless.

The trash can beside the refrigerator is filled to the brim with empty food containers. Mills begins to poke around with a pen.

O'NEILL

You girls have got forensics waiting outside. I don't know if we'll all fit, though.

MILLS

There's room. Light's the problem.

Somerset looks at Mills, then at the space limitations.

> SOMERSET

Two is company here.
> (*pause*)

Detective Mills, go help the officers question the neighbors.

Mills looks up, not pleased.

> MILLS

I'll stay on this.

Somerset is looking at the corpse.

> SOMERSET

Send one of the forensics in on your way out.

Mills does not move. He lifts his flashlight to shine the light on the side of Somerset's face. A moment. Somerset looks at Mills, the light shining directly in Somerset's eyes. A longer moment. Mills switches off the light and leaves.

O'Neill places both hands on the dead man's head and lifts the swollen visage from the spaghetti.

> O'NEILL

He's dead.

> SOMERSET

Thank you, doctor.

INT. SOMERSET'S CAR – DAY

Somerset drives; Mills sits in the passenger seat. Heavy city traffic. Both stare ahead in silence. Mills is a bundle of nerves.

> MILLS

You've seen my files, right? Seen the things I've done?

> SOMERSET

No.

> MILLS
> (*looking out window*)

Anyway . . . I did my time on door-to-doors, and walking a beat. I did all that shit for a long time.

SOMERSET

Good.

MILLS

The badge in my pocket says 'detective', same as yours.

SOMERSET

I made a decision. I have to consider the integrity of the
scene. I can't worry whether you think you're getting enough
time on the playing field.

MILLS

Yeah, well, all I want is . . .
(*pause*)
Just, just don't be jerking me off. That's all I ask. Don't jerk
me off.

*Mills looks at Somerset. Somerset keeps his eyes on the road, but nods
slightly. That said, Mills slumps low into his seat.*

SOMERSET

We'll be spending every waking hour together till I leave. I'll
show you your friends and enemies. I'll help you cut through
red tape. I'll help you 'integrate', as the captain puts it.
However . . .
(*pause, clears throat*)
No matter how you beg or plead . . . jerking off is something
you'll have to do for yourself.

This throws Mills. Somerset has a sense of humor?

I don't think we should have that sort of relationship. We'd
start quarreling over insignificant things.

Mills lets out a nervous laugh, feels a bit of weight off his shoulders.

MILLS

Whatever you say, Detective. Beautiful.

INT. AUTOPSY ROOM – DAY

*The room is large, cold and clean. Stainless steel and white tile. Many
pathologists work at slabs. A bone saw screams. Mills and Somerset are*

with DOCTOR SANTIAGO, who stands over the obese corpse which is pretty well dissected already.

SANTIAGO

He's been dead for a long time, and I can tell you it was not a poison.

Santiago moves to make room for Mills to stand beside him.

Mills moves up a little, but not much, looking on in disgust. Santiago reaches into the man's belly, moving something. There is a squashy sound. We do not see.

MILLS

Ah, man . . . how does somebody let himself go like that?

SANTIAGO

It took four orderlies just to put this body on the table.

Somerset leans to peer into many jars on a table. A few organs and various unidentifiable blobs of mush are contained in fluid. Somerset leans closer.

In one jar of pulp, two small, BLUE FLECKS float in the preserving fluid. Somerset taps the jar with his finger.

MILLS

How did that fat fuck ever fit out the door of his apartment?

SOMERSET

Please. It's obvious he was a shut in.

SANTIAGO

Are you looking here? First . . . see how big this stomach is.

Somerset turns his attention back to the corpse.

And, see the strange thing. Stretches. And, here . . . look at the size of that, because of all the foods.

MILLS

I can see what you're pointing at, but . . .

SANTIAGO

Lines of distention across the stomach, and parts have ripped open.

SOMERSET

This man ate till he burst?

SANTIAGO

Well, he didn't really burst. Not all the way. But, he was bleeding inside himself, and there was a hematoma on the outside . . .

(*points to it*)

. . . on the belly. Very large.

Somerset walks around the slab, looking down at the obese man's propped-up, partially shaven head.

MILLS

He died by eating?

SANTIAGO

Yes.

SOMERSET

These bruises . . .

On the victim's head, more round and semi-circular bruises have been revealed, all about the same diameter as a dime.

SANTIAGO

I don't know what they are yet. They . . .

SOMERSET

The muzzle of a gun . . . pressed against the back of his head.

Santiago comes to look, nodding.

SANTIAGO

It's possible, if it was pushed against hard enough, sure.

Mills leans close to the bruises, squinting. He points with his pinkie finger, without touching.

MILLS

Christ . . . marks from the front sight, flush with the muzzle.

Mills stands straight, eyes excited, almost pleased.

Ladies and gentlemen . . . we have a homicide.

Somerset doesn't share his enthusiasm.

INT. PRECINCT HOUSE. CAPTAIN'S OFFICE – EARLY EVENING

The Captain's office is filled with books and mug sheets. Piles of paperwork abound. The CAPTAIN, 50, sits at his desk. He's a calm man, but whenever he is not speaking, he clenches his jaw over and over without fail, causing the muscles in his neck and jaw to pulse. Somerset and Mills sit before him.

> SOMERSET
>
> He was given a choice. Eat, or your brains blown out. He ate his fill, and was forced to continue.

Somerset gets up to pace.

> The killer held a bucket under him and kept serving. Took his time. The coroner says this might have gone on for more than twelve hours. The victim's throat was swollen, probably from the effort, and there was definitely a point where he passed out. That's when killer kicked him. Popped him.

> MILLS
>
> Sadistic motherfucker.

> SOMERSET
>
> This was premeditated in the extreme. This whole thing is a statement.

> CAPTAIN
>
> Hold on . . . Somebody had a gripe with the fat boy and decided to torture him . . .

> SOMERSET
>
> No. You want someone dead, you walk in and shoot them. You don't risk the time it takes to do this unless the act itself has meaning. We found two grocery receipts, which means the killer stopped in the middle of everything and made a second trip to the supermarket.

The Captain is disgruntled, clenching his jaw. He looks to Mills.

> MILLS
>
> It's his stuff, man. I've been out in the cold all day.

23

SOMERSET

This is beginning.

CAPTAIN

Always working up there, huh, Somerset? Big brain's always
cooking.

Somerset sits.

SOMERSET

I want to be reassigned.

MILLS

Whoa, whoa . . . what?

CAPTAIN

What are you talking about?

SOMERSET

This can't be my last duty here. It will go on and on.

CAPTAIN

You're retiring. In six days you're all the way gone.

Somerset shakes his head.

You've left unfinished business before.

SOMERSET

Everything else was taken as close to conclusion as humanly
possible. Also, if you want my opinion . . . it shouldn't be his
first assignment.

Mills stands, furious.

MILLS

This isn't my first assignment, dickhead. What the hell?

SOMERSET

This is too soon for him.

MILLS

Hey, I'm right here. Say it to my face.

CAPTAIN

Sit down, Mills.

MILLS
(*to Captain*)
Can we talk about this in private? It's not like I was begging to
work with this guy . . .

CAPTAIN
Just sit.

Mills does. The Captain scratches his face, sighs.

I don't have anyone else to give this to, Somerset, you know
that. Nobody's going to *swap* with you.

MILLS
Give it to me.

CAPTAIN
How's that?

MILLS
He wants out, 'goodbye'. Give it to me.

The Captain considers this, looks to Somerset. Pause.

CAPTAIN
(*to Mills*)
I'm putting you on something else. Go down the hall. We'll
shuffle papers and find a new partner.

Mills looks at Somerset, then leaves, closing the door.

CAPTAIN
You're stuck with the fat man. Clean up as much as possible.
Stop making it into more than it is.

Somerset seems deflated, staring at the floor.

That's all, Somerset. You're excused.

INSERT – TITLE CARD: TUESDAY

EXT. UPSCALE CITY STREET – MORNING

*A newspaper vendor lays out a pile of tabloid newspapers at the front of
his busy news-stand. The paper's headline is:* BIZARRE
MURDER!, *in huge, black print.*

The vendor lays out another tabloid pile. Headline: 'EAT OR DIE'
SAYS FAT MAN KILLER!! *in big, red letters.*

The vendor throws down a third tabloid stack. It reads:
SICKENING MURDER – EXCLUSIVE DETAILS
INSIDE!

INT. PRECINCT HOUSE. SOMERSET'S OFFICE – DAY

*The office is old, with a single window which faces a billboard.
TRAFFIC is HEARD from outside. There are moving boxes on the
floor. Somerset is at his desk with paperwork in two sloppy piles. He
uses a manual typewriter, filling in a yellow form. He types hunt-and-
peck, slowly. He finishes the form and pulls it out. There is a knock at
the door.*

                    SOMERSET
    Come in.

*The Captain pushes the door and stands in the doorway with a
PAINTER/WORKMAN at his side.*

                    CAPTAIN
    Pardon us. We have some business to take care of.

As always, the Captain clenches his jaw.

Somerset lines a new form in the typewriter, begins typing.

*The Captain strolls in. Two boxes sit on the floor with DETECTIVE
MILLS written across them. He picks up one of the boxes and sets it on
top of the other.*

*At the open door, the Workman takes a razor blade from his kit. He
brings it against the writing on the glass of the door: DETECTIVE
SOMERSET. The workman pushes the razor to start scraping the name
away, and the razor on glass sounds like fingernails on a blackboard.*

Somerset looks up.

                    WORKMAN
    Sorry.

*Somerset turns back to the typing, hunt-and-peck. The Captain
watches. The Workman continues.*

CAPTAIN

Have you heard?

SOMERSET

No, I haven't heard.

Somerset just keeps typing.

CAPTAIN

Eli Gould was found murdered.

Somerset stops, looks at the Captain.

Someone broke into his law office and bled him to death.
Wrote the word 'greed' on the ceiling in his blood.

SOMERSET

Greed?

CAPTAIN

Mills is heading the investigation.

Somerset thinks about this, then turns to type.

SOMERSET

I'm sure everyone's doing their best.

CAPTAIN

Yeah.

SOMERSET

Good.

*Hunt-and-peck. The Captain's jowls clamp shut. He starts to straighten
two piles of forms on Somerset's desk.*

CAPTAIN

What are you going to do with yourself out there, Somerset?

SOMERSET

I'll get a job, maybe on a farm. I'll work on the house.

CAPTAIN

Can't you feel it yet? Can't you feel that feeling . . .? You're
not going to be a cop anymore.

SOMERSET

Yes, that's the whole point.

CAPTAIN

Come on. You're not leaving.

Somerset reclines, facing the Captain.

SOMERSET

A man is walking his dog at night. He's attacked. His wallet
and his watch are taken. While he's still lying unconscious,
his attacker stabs him with a knife in both eyes. That
happened, last night, about four blocks from here.

CAPTAIN

I read about it.

SOMERSET

I have no understanding of this place anymore.

CAPTAIN

It's always been like this.

SOMERSET

Really?

Somerset saddles up to the typewriter.

Maybe you're right.

The Captain lays the paperwork down. Both piles are now neat.

CAPTAIN

You do this work. You were made for it, and I don't think
you can deny that. I certainly can't believe you're trading it in
for a tool belt and a fishing rod.

(*pause*)

Maybe I'm wrong.

*He takes a jar from his pocket. Inside are small pieces of blue plastic,
curled slightly, as if they are scrapings.*

This is for you. The coroner found them in the fat man's
stomach, in with the food. Looks like little pieces of plastic.

Thank you. Put them there.

The Captain puts the jar down on the desk. He leaves.

Somerset looks up. He grabs the paperwork piles and ruffles them back to their disheveled state. He picks up the jar. He looks in at the plastic pieces, shakes it.

Somerset gets up and heads to leave, passing the Workman who has a rag in his hand to remove the last remnants of Somerset's name.

SOMERSET
(*angrily*)
Try putting a little elbow grease into it.

The Workman is startled. Somerset heads down the hallway.

INT. APARTMENT BUILDING. HALLWAY – DAY

The door to the apartment where the fat man was found murdered. Somerset uses his switchblade to cut the 'crime scene' tape sealing the seam of the door. He enters.

INT. APARTMENT. KITCHEN – DAY

The room where the obese corpse was found. Somerset enters, flicks the light switch and gets fluorescent light. The place has been dusted for prints. Somerset takes the jar from his pocket, looking around.

He looks to the ceiling. Walks around the kitchen table. He looks at the floor, then holds up the jar for study.

He gets down, holds the jar against the linoleum. Blue. Like the plastic scrapings. Same color and texture. Somerset shakes his head, finding this strange.

On his hands and knees, he searches the surface of the floor, examining every nick. He's moving towards the refrigerator.

Somerset stops. There are deep scratches here in the linoleum. He fingers the grooves, then takes a piece of the plastic from the jar. He holds the piece to the floor, fiddles . . . fits it into one of the scratches.

Somerset stands, looking down. These scratches are in front of the refrigerator, like they were caused by the refrigerator having been pulled away from the wall and pushed back into place.

Somerset grips the refrigerator, pulling it. It isn't easy. He has to shift it a little at a time, rocking it back and forth.

The refrigerator's coming forward. Sweat forms on Somerset's face as he finally pushes from the side of the refrigerator, clearing the way for a view of the wall behind.

Somerset leans to look, numbed by what he sees.

> SOMERSET

Oh Lord . . .

There is a space on the wall where dust has been wiped away. In that space, the word: GLUTTONY. The letters have been smeared on in grease. A hand-written note is pinned beside them.

INT. PRECINCT HOUSE. CAPTAIN'S OFFICE – DAY

Somerset reads the note, which is sealed inside an evidence bag.

> SOMERSET

'Long is the way, and hard, that out of hell leads up to light.'

Mills stands, brooding, hands in his pockets. The Captain is behind his desk. Somerset lays the note down.

There are seven deadly sins. Gluttony, greed, wrath, envy, sloth, pride and lust. Seven.

The Captain stares at the note. PHONE RINGS. He picks it up and punches a button. Somerset looks at Mills, then heads for the door.

> CAPTAIN

Hold on, Somerset . . .
> *(into phone)*
Yeah? I'll get back to you, alright?

The Captain hangs up, looks to Somerset in the doorway.

Somerset . . .

No. He wanted it. I don't . . . I can't have anything to do
with this.

*The Captain looks at Somerset as Somerset waits. Finally the Captain
motions for him to go. He does. The door shuts.*

END OF ACT I

INT. SOMERSET'S CAR – EARLY EVENING

*Somerset drives, slow, in a traffic jam. He stares at the cars ahead. He
reaches to turn on the RADIO. MUSIC PLAYS quietly.*

*Somerset just keeps staring forward through the windshield. After a
moment, he reaches to TURN the RADIO off. Stares ahead.*

INT. SOMERSET'S APARTMENT. LIVING-ROOM – LATE NIGHT

*There is a dartboard on one wall. Thwack – Somerset's switchblade hits
the board and embeds.*

*Somerset crosses the nearly empty living-room and takes the blade from
the dartboard. He walks back to stand in front of the only chair in the
room. He throws the switchblade.*

It embeds in the dartboard. Somerset sits.

*He picks a book off the floor and holds it in his lap. Kids can be
HEARD CURSING and playing LOUD MUSIC from outside the
shuttered window. Somerset stares at the ceiling. He opens the book and
looks at the pages . . . Stares at the pages . . .*

He puts the book back down on the floor.

EXT. CITY STREET – LATE NIGHT

*Somerset gets out of his car. He walks down the sidewalk with a
notebook in hand. THUNDER is HEARD. He takes a cigarette out of
a full pack and lights it.*

*He walks along the avenue. Cars race by in the street. People walk
briskly past. At a public phone, a man shouts curses angrily into the
phone, then starts pounding the phone box with the receiver. A fire-
engine passes in the street, sirens, horn and lights going full blast.*

Somerset starts up a flight of massive stone stairs, past several sleeping vagrants. One VAGRANT sits up and looks to Somerset.

> VAGRANT
>
> Spare me a cigarette? Spare a cigarette?

> SOMERSET
>
> Sorry, last one.

Ahead of Somerset, the library looms, a solid, powerful structure.

INT. PUBLIC LIBRARY. MAIN LIBRARY – LATE NIGHT

Somerset and GEORGE, 62, the night guard, enter the vast space of the deserted main library. The lamps hanging from the ceiling give off a warm, pleasant glow over mahogany tables and chairs. To each side of this center area are tall bookshelves. Balconies surround the room on all four sides; three levels overlook the center.

Somerset is happy. This is his element, this peaceful, elegant place. George motions to the long, empty tables.

> GEORGE
>
> Sit where you'd like.

> SOMERSET
>
> Thanks, George.

> MAN'S VOICE
> (*off-screen*)
>
> Hey there, Smiley.

Somerset looks up to the top balcony where TWO OTHER SECURITY GUARDS and one JANITOR look over the banister.

> SOMERSET
>
> Evening.

They all say their hellos.

> FIRST GUARD
>
> Come on, George. Cards are getting cold.

GEORGE
(*to Somerset*)

Duty calls.

George pumps Somerset's hand, then moves to a stairwell leading to the balconies. Somerset walks down the main aisle, looks around at the shelves and shelves of books.

George reaches the top balcony and the others sit at a card table where a poker game is in progress.

Somerset puts his notebook down on one table and switches on a green banker's lamp. THUNDER SOUNDS. Somerset looks up.

Rain is beginning to fall on the windows of the high ceiling.

SOMERSET
(*shouts up*)

All these books, gentlemen . . . A world of knowledge at your disposal, and you play poker all night.

UP ON THE BALCONY George has taken a huge boom-box from a broom closet.

JANITOR

We got culture.

SECOND GUARD
(*dealing cards*)

Yeah, we got culture coming out our asses.

They laugh. George sets the boom-box against the railing of the balcony so the speakers face towards Somerset.

DOWN ON THE MAIN FLOOR Somerset has gone into one bookshelf aisle. Poker table conversation echoes from above. Somerset searches books, reading spines. He finds one book and pulls it, continues searching.

UP ON THE BALCONY George hits play on the boom-box and turns the volume way up.

GEORGE

How's this for culture?

DOWN ON THE MAIN FLOOR Somerset keeps looking for books. From far away the strains of MOZART MUSIC fills the air. High, drifting music, such as Bach's 'Air on a G string'. Somerset stops, listens.

He closes his eyes and soaks it in.

UP ON THE BALCONY George sits at the card table, takes out a cigar and lights up. He looks to the ground floor.

                    GEORGE
    Where'd you get to, Smiley?

Below, Somerset comes out from the aisle.

DOWN ON THE MAIN FLOOR Somerset looks up at George.

                    SOMERSET
    Thank you.

INT. PUBLIC LIBRARY. MAIN LIBRARY – LATER – NIGHT

MUSIC CONTINUES, spinning through the air like a slow, cool breeze.

Somerset walks, surrounded by books, carrying several. He pulls another off a shelf and adds it to his pile.

UP ON THE BALCONY George lays down a winning hand. The others toss in their cards in disgust. George laughs, spouting cigar smoke.

Cigar smoke floats up in the air, thinning gracefully. Above, rain continues dancing on the ceiling windows.

DOWN ON THE MAIN FLOOR Somerset sits, opens a book on the table and reads.

INT. MILLS' APARTMENT. BEDROOM/LIVING-ROOM – NIGHT

Music continues uninterrupted over this scene; music so pretty it is almost sad. Tracy, in a nightgown, sits up in bed, tense. She throws off the covers and goes to the door.

She stands looking into the living-room where Mills is at a desk.

Mills sorts through paperwork and photos with his back to Tracy. A

34

basketball game is on the television, but he pays it no attention. He sits forward, obviously frustrated, drinks coffee. He does not know Tracy is there.

Tracy watches her husband, concerned.

INT. PUBLIC LIBRARY. MAIN LIBRARY – NIGHT

MUSIC CONTINUES. Somerset has two books open. He opens his notebook and brings a pen to bear. Writes:

SEVEN DEADLY SINS
GLUTTONY GREED WRATH LUST PRIDE ENVY SLOTH

He crosses out GLUTTONY and GREED.

Somerset picks up one book: Dante's Purgatory. *Volume II of the* Divine Comedy. *Somerset opens it:*

UP ON THE BALCONY George and the guys finish another hand. George looks down at Somerset, who is writing in the notebook.

George takes up the cards and starts shuffling.

> GEORGE
> (*down to Somerset*)
> You know, Smiley . . . you're really going to miss us.

George shuffles again, but they flip wrong and a few go off the table, over the balcony.

DOWN ON THE MAIN FLOOR Somerset looks up at George, then looks around.

> SOMERSET
> I just might.

ABOVE, the cards George dropped are fluttering, flipping downwards.

INT. PRECINCT HOUSE. SOMERSET'S OFFICE – EARLY EVENING

The office is dark. Somerset is at his desk, writing:

> *Detective Mills,*
> You may want to look at the following books, relating to the *Seven Deadly Sins*:

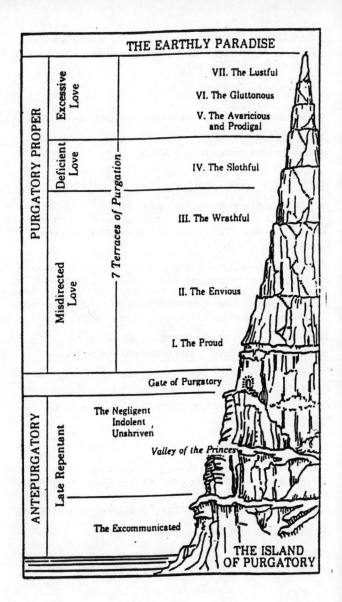

THE EARTHLY PARADISE

PURGATORY PROPER

Excessive Love
VII. The Lustful
VI. The Gluttonous
V. The Avaricious and Prodigal

Deficient Love
IV. The Slothful

Misdirected Love
III. The Wrathful
II. The Envious
I. The Proud

7 Terraces of Purgation

Gate of Purgatory

ANTEPURGATORY

Late Repentant
The Negligent
Indolent
Unshriven

Valley of the Princes

The Excommunicated

THE ISLAND OF PURGATORY

Dante's *Purgatory*
The Canterbury Tales – The Parson's Tale
Dictionary of Catholicism

INT. PRECINCT HOUSE. SOMERSET'S OFFICE – LATER – EVENING

Somerset lays an envelope on top of the two boxes which have Detective Mills' name on them. The envelope reads: MILLS.

INSERT – TITLE CARD: WEDNESDAY

INT. PRECINCT HOUSE. SOMERSET'S OFFICE – MORNING

Somerset pushes the door open and notices 'DETECTIVE MILLS' painted on the glass. Rain falls outside. Somerset goes to his desk, but stops. All his belongings have been moved to a small, temporary desk in the corner.

Somerset moves to open the top left drawer of the big desk. Empty.

He goes to the temporary desk and urgently searches through the boxes of papers and files . . . finds what he was looking for. He holds a small frame which fits in his palm.

Inside the frame is a PHOTO of an attractive WOMAN. Somerset pops the frame open, looks at the picture, then puts the picture in his wallet.

Somerset sits at the temporary desk. He begins to sort through his papers. After a moment, he glances over his shoulder. The envelope he left for Mills is gone.

INT. UPSCALE BUILDING. STAIRWELL – MORNING

The door into an ugly stairwell bangs open and a reporter and cameraman run in, hurrying up the stairs. The cameraman turns on his bright floodlight. A COMMOTION ECHOES from above. Mills enters from this same door, in no hurry, looking haggard.

Mills climbs the stairs. Up a few floors.

Ahead of him, there's a crowded, frantic press conference of sorts taking place on a landing. Reporters and camera people jockey for positions around MARTIN TALBOT, 47, a smartly dressed, impressive figure with a gold tooth in the front of his mouth. FLASHBULBS FLASH. Talbot tries to quell overlapping questions.

> TALBOT

One at a time, please. One at a time.
> > (*pointing to reporter*)

You there.

Mills has to squeeze through the crush of bodies.

> REPORTER
> > (*to Talbot, with glee*)

Mr Talbot, can you confirm any of the rumors that Mr Gould was forced to mutilate himself?

> TALBOT

I can't address any of the specifics while the investigation is still ongoing. Weren't you listening when I said that before?

Mills gets past, moving on. QUESTIONS are SHOUTED at Talbot. One NEWSWOMAN with a mini-recorder breaks off from the group to follow Mills.

> NEWSWOMAN

Detective . . . Detective, can I have a moment of your time?

> MILLS

No.

Mills keeps going. The woman watches him, looks back to Talbot and decides he's more important, hurrying back down.

FOLLOW Mills. He pushes through another door, into . . .

INT. UPSCALE BUILDING. SERVICE AREA – MORNING

A dark physical plant room. Mills crosses past humming air-conditioning units, dripping pipes and janitorial lockers to a door . . .

INT. UPSCALE BUILDING. OFFICE CORRIDOR – MORNING

Mills comes out the service area door into a bright, ritzy hallway. This hall and the doors along it reek of money. A few cops and rent-a-cops are standing around near a portion of the hall that's been blocked off by a POLICE LINE saw horse.

Mills passes, nodding to the cops. He heads left, into another hall, around a corner, through an open door . . .

. . . INTO A BOARDROOM. Several forensics sort and label plastic bags of evidence spread out across the vast meeting table. A photographer loads equipment. Mills crosses to an adjoining . . .

. . . KITCHENETTE. Other cops brush past on their way out. The kitchenette leads to a small SECRETARIAL OFFICE. Mills moves to a huge mahogany door . . .

INT. LAW OFFICE – MORNING

Mills enters. Huge law office with windows overlooking the wet city. TV in a corner shows the news. Two whispering FORENSICS are on ladders, dusting for prints around the word 'GREED' on the ceiling in blood.

> FORENSIC ONE
> *(to other forensic)*
> . . . going to screw it up, I swear. Fucking kid. Can't be more than . . .

The other forensic clears his throat, getting back to work. Forensic One shuts up. Mills notices this, weary.

> MILLS
> How's it coming?

> FORENSIC ONE
> Nothing yet, boss.

Mills watches them a moment, then turns his attention to another part of the office. He walks.

A leather chair sits in an open area. The chair and the carpet under it are covered in lots of brown, dried blood.

There is a trail of dripped blood from the chair to a big desk in front of a large, abstract modern art painting on the wall.

On a cleared-off section of the desk, a two-armed, counter balance SCALE sits, also blood-stained. The desk has been dusted.

Mills stands staring at this. The TELEVISION is HEARD:

ANCHOR
(voice-over; from television)
. . . going to cut live to downtown, where Defense Attorney
Eli Gould was found murdered in his office early Tuesday
morning. District Attorney Martin Talbot is now taking
questions from reporters . . .

On TV, Talbot comes on screen. It's from the stairwell.

A REPORTER
(voice-over; from television)
. . . a conflict of interest here? I mean, your prosecutors have
lost more than a few very high-profile cases to Mr Gould and
his defense team . . .

TALBOT
(voice-over; from television)
Now, that's ridiculous to the point of being offensive. There's
no conflict whatsoever and any claim that there would be, or
could be, is irresponsible.

Other reporters begin to shout questions, but Talbot's not done.

Now, hold on . . . I want to address that. I've just come from
a meeting with law enforcement officials, and they've assured
me they put their best people on this thing.

Mills turns to look at Talbot on the screen.

This will be the very definition of swift justice.

Mills walks to turn off the TV.

MILLS
(quietly to TV)
Shut the fuck up.

*He turns and looks to see the forensics looking at him. The forensics look
away.*

*Mills walks away from the TV towards a picture frame on the floor.
The frame has been placed specifically in the center of the room, facing
the main doors.*

It is a photo of a falsely pretty, middle-aged woman, smiling and wearing pearls. On the glass of the frame, two circles have been drawn with blood around the woman's eyes.

Mills sits on the floor. He stares at the photo.

INT. MILLS' CAR – MORNING

Mills gets in and slams the door. He is alone with the sound of the rain. He wipes water from his face and looks at his tired eyes in the rear-view mirror. He leans over to the glove compartment and takes out two newly purchased paperbacks: The Canterbury Tales *and Dante's* Purgatory.

Mills makes a face and opens Dante's Purgatory *to a bookmark. He rests the book on the steering-wheel. He reads.*

He bites his lip, leaning close to the words.

He's really concentrating, mouths some of it to himself. He finally shakes his head and closes the book, not understanding a word. Pause. He starts pounding the book against the steering-wheel with all his might.

> MILLS
> Fucking, Dante, goddamn, poetry-writing, faggot motherfucker . . .

Mills throws the book against the windshield, then puts his head back and closes his eyes, trying to calm. A long moment. Quiet. BANG, BANG, BANG – there's a loud BANGING on the window and Mills looks up, startled . . .

A tall cop is at the window in rain gear. Mills rolls it down. Tall cop hands a wet paper bag through.

> Good work, Officer. Good work.

Mills rolls the window up, rips the bag open. Inside: Cliff's Notes *for Dante's* Purgatory *and for* The Canterbury Tales.

> Thank God.

INT. PRECINCT HOUSE. SOMERSET'S OFFICE – DAY

It still rains outside. Somerset sits at the big desk which is now Mills'.

He fills out forms by hand as Mills enters with a ton of his own paperwork. Somerset looks up.

SOMERSET
(*gathers his things*)
Let me get out of your way.

Mills sets his paperwork on the desk. He is beat. Somerset moves to the temporary desk. They both sit and settle in, organizing, not looking at each other.

Both attend to their work. Here are two men, about five feet apart, each trying not to acknowledge the other's presence. Mills takes his Cliff's Notes *out, looks to check that Somerset is occupied, and hides them in a desk drawer.*

Somerset finishes one form, flips it and looks at Mills. Mills sorts through photos from the greed murder. Somerset continues writing. PHONE RINGS. Both men look at it. Phone rings again.

SOMERSET
It's a package deal. You get the phone with the office.

MILLS
(*picks up, into phone*)
Detective Mills.
(*concerned, lowers voice*)
Honey, hi. What's wrong? Is everything okay?
(*listens*)
Well . . . didn't I ask you not to call me here? I'm working . . .
(*listens*)
What? Why?

Mills is very confused.
(*into phone*)
Why? Okay . . . okay, hold on.

Mills clears his throat and holds out the phone to Somerset.

It's my wife.

SOMERSET
What?

Mills shrugs. Somerset stands, takes the phone.
                    (*into phone*)
        Hello?
                    (*listens*)
        Yes, well . . . it's nice to speak to you.
                    (*listens*)
        Well, I appreciate the thought . . . but . . .
                    (*listens*)
        Then, I guess I'd be delighted. Thank you very much. Yes
        . . . goodbye.

Somerset hangs up, shakes his head.

                    MILLS
        Well?

                    SOMERSET
        I'm invited to have a late supper at your house. And, I accept.

                    MILLS
        How's that?

                    SOMERSET
        Tonight.

Mills is lost. Somerset goes to sit back down.

                    MILLS
        I don't even know if *I'm* having dinner there tonight.

INT. MILLS' APARTMENT. LIVING-ROOM/KITCHENETTE – NIGHT

*Food is cooking on the stove. Tracy is in the living-room area carefully
setting the table with good silver and china.*

*The door of the apartment is HEARD OPENING and CLOSING.
Mills and Somerset come down a short hallway. Mills carries a brand-
new briefcase.*

                    TRACY
        Hello, men. You made it.

                    MILLS
        Hi, honey.

Mills gives Tracy a kiss, then presents Somerset.

I'd like you to meet Somerset.

SOMERSET

Hello.

Somerset shakes Tracy's hand lightly.

TRACY

It's nice to meet you. My husband has told me a lot about you . . . except your first name.

SOMERSET

Oh . . . um, William.

TRACY

It's a nice name. William, I'd like you to meet David.
(*to Mills*)
David . . . William.

Mills smiles and nods this off, heading across the room.

MILLS

Great . . . I'm, uh, just going to put these things away.

Mills moves to an adjoining room. As soon as he opens the door, his DOGS are BARKING. Mills has to block their escape with his body. He greets them with kissing sounds as he shuts the door.

Somerset stands with his hands folded in front of him.

SOMERSET

It smells good.

TRACY

What? Oh, yes. I mean, thank you.
(*motions to table*)
Please, sit down.

Somerset takes off his jacket. Tracy goes to check on the food.

You can put that over on the couch. You'll have to excuse all the mess. We're still unpacking.

Somerset notices something on Mills' desk. It's a medal, in a small, clear case among the papers and pens.

SOMERSET

I hear you two were high-school sweethearts.

TRACY

High school and college, yes. Pretty hokey, huh? I knew on our first date this was the man I was going to marry. God . . . he was the funniest guy I'd ever met.

SOMERSET

Really?

Somerset has to think about that one for a second. He picks the medal up: a medal for valor from the Police Department.

Well, it's rare these days . . . that kind of commitment.

He puts the medal down. Tracy is looking at the gun strapped under Somerset's arm as Somerset starts to unstrap it.

(*about the gun*)

Don't worry. I don't wear it at the dinner table.

TRACY

No matter how often I see guns, I still can't get used to them.

Somerset lays the gun with his jacket.

SOMERSET

Same here.

Tracy smiles. Somerset goes to the table and transfers a small notebook from his breast pocket to his pants pocket. A piece of paper falls to the floor, closer to Tracy.

TRACY

Anyway . . . what girl wouldn't want the captain of the football team as their lifetime mate? Here . . . you dropped something . . .

Tracy picks it up. It is the pale, paper rose. She looks at it as she hands it back to Somerset, who is self-conscious.

What is that?

Somerset looks at the rose, then puts it away.

SOMERSET

My future.

Tracy tilts her head, looking at Somerset.

TRACY

You have a strange way about you . . . I mean interesting. I'm
sorry. It's really none of my business. It's just nice, to meet a
man who talks like . . .
                    (*trails off, goes back to stove*)
If David saw that paper, he'd say you're a fag. That's how he
is.

SOMERSET
                    (*smiles*)
I guess I won't be showing it to him then.

INT. MILLS' APARTMENT. LIVING-ROOM – LATER NIGHT

*A record-player on a moving box PLAYS QUIET MUSIC. Tracy,
Mills and Somerset are eating. Mills has a beeper beside his plate and
occasionally fingers it absently.*

TRACY

Why aren't you married, William?

MILLS

Tracy . . . what the hell?

Somerset pokes at his napkin, thinking.

SOMERSET

I was close once. It just didn't happen.

TRACY

It surprises me. It really does.

SOMERSET

Any person who spends a significant amount of time with me
finds me . . . disagreeable. Just ask your husband.

MILLS

Very true.

Mills grins, but he means it.

46

TRACY
(to Somerset)
How long have you lived here?

SOMERSET
Too long.
(drinks)
How do you like it?

Tracy glances immediately to Mills.

MILLS
It takes time to settle in.

Somerset can see it is a sore subject.

SOMERSET
Well, you get numb to it pretty quickly. There are things in any city . . .

A LOW RUMBLING is HEARD. Plates on the table begin to clatter.

MILLS
Subway train.

The dishes clatter more. Coffee cups clink against their saucers. Tracy holds her coffee cup to stop it and smiles at Somerset, acting like it's nothing, but she is clearly bothered.

TRACY
It'll go away in a minute.

They wait. The rumbling grows louder, knocks something over in the sink. The DOGS are HEARD WHINING and HOWLING from the other room. Somerset continues eating, fiddles with his food.

The record-player skips, then plays on. The clattering begins to die down. The dogs quiet. Mills seems uncomfortable.

MILLS
This real estate guy . . . this miserable fuck, he brought us to see this place a few times. And, first I'm thinking he's good, really efficient. But then, I started wondering, why does he keep hurrying us along? Why will he only show us this place for like five minutes at a time?

Mills laughs lamely.

> TRACY
>
> We found out the first night.

Somerset tries to stay straight, but he can't help laughing.

> SOMERSET
>
> The soothing, relaxing, vibrating home. Sorry . . .

He laughs harder, covering his mouth. Tracy and Mills laugh.

> MILLS
>
> Oh, fuck.

INT. MILLS' APARTMENT. LIVING-ROOM – LATER NIGHT

The record-player plays another album. Tracy brings over a pot of coffee and pours. Mills and Somerset have beers.

> TRACY
>
> I don't think I've ever met anyone who doesn't have a television before. That's . . . weird.

> MILLS
>
> It's un-American is what it is.

> SOMERSET
>
> All television does is teach children that it's okay to be stupid and eat candy bars all day.

> MILLS
>
> What about sports?

> SOMERSET
>
> What about them?

Tracy brings over a plate of cookies and puts it on the table.

> MILLS
>
> You go to movies at least?

> SOMERSET
>
> I read.

MILLS

I just have to say, I can't respect any man who's never seen *Green Acres*.

Somerset gives a blank stare. Tracy walks across the room.

You've *never* seen *The Odd Couple*? This is sick. *The Honeymooners*?!

SOMERSET

I vaguely recall a large, angry man named Norton.

Tracy turns the record-player down further, then goes into the bedroom and shuts the door behind her.

Somerset and Mills look at the closed door. A long moment. They look at each other, then sit for a time. Somerset puts down his beer, sighs. He looks around.

INT. MILLS' APARTMENT. LIVING-ROOM – LATER – NIGHT

The only sounds are from the city outside. The living-room table has been cleared and its surface is now covered with various forms, reports and 8" by 10" photographs. Mills and Somerset are both standing. Mills guides Somerset through the photos.

MILLS

Our guy got into the office, probably before the building closed and security tightened up. Gould must have been working late.

SOMERSET

I'm certain. He was the biggest defense lawyer around. Infamous, actually.

MILLS

Well, his body was found Tuesday morning, okay? But, get this . . . The office was closed all day Monday. Which means as long as the gluttony killing was done before the weekend, our killer could've gotten in here Friday. He could've spent all day Saturday with Gould, and Sunday and maybe even Monday.

Mills picks up one photo and shows it to Somerset. Long shot: it shows

49

*the greed murder scene. Gould sits dead in the leather chair, near the
desk where the counter-balance scale sits.*

Gould was tied down, nude. The killer left his arms free and
handed him a big, sharp butcher's knife. See . . . the scale
here.

*Mills pulls another photo. Close-up: the two-armed scale. In one
suspended plate is a one-pound weight.*

In the other is a hunk of flesh.

SOMERSET

A pound of flesh.

Mills digs, comes up with a photocopy of a hand-scrawled note.

(*reading note*)
'One pound of flesh, no more no less. No cartilage, no bone,
but only flesh. This task done . . . and he would go free.'

Mills takes out one photo showing the note pinned to the wall.

MILLS

The leather chair was soaked through with sweat.

SOMERSET
(*nods, grim*)
All day Saturday, Sunday and Monday.
(*pause*)
The murderer would want Gould to take his time. To have to
sit there and decide. Where do you make the first cut?
There's a gun in your face . . . but, what part of your body is
expendable?

MILLS

He cut along the side of his stomach. The love handle.

Somerset begins spreading the photos out in front of him.

SOMERSET

Look at these with fresh eyes. Don't let the killer guide
you . . .

50

As he speaks, Somerset keeps shifting the photos; covering the corpse in one with the edge of another, editing each by overlapping with another.

Even if the corpse is right there . . . it's almost like looking through it. Editing out the initial shock. You always have to find one singular thing to focus on. There's always one thing, and it may be as small as a speck of dust, but you find it and focus . . . till it's an exhausted possibility.

In the photos, there's the scale. The note on the wall. Shelves of books. The abstract, modern art painting.

GREED *written in blood.*

> SOMERSET

He's preaching.

> MILLS

Punishing.

> SOMERSET

The sins were used in medieval sermons. There were seven cardinal virtues, and then seven deadly sins, created as a learning tool, because they distract from true worship.

> MILLS

Like in *The Parson's Tale* and Dante.

> SOMERSET

You read them?

> MILLS

Yeah. Well, parts of them. Anyway, in *Purgatory*, Dante and his buddy are climbing up that big mountain . . . seeing all these other guys who sinned . . .

> SOMERSET

Seven Terraces of Purgation.

> MILLS

Right. But there, pride comes first, not gluttony. The sins are in a different order.

> SOMERSET

For now, just consider the books as the murderer's

inspiration. The books and sermons are about atonement for sin. And, these murders have been like forced attrition.

                    MILLS
Forced what?

                    SOMERSET
Attrition. When you regret your sins, but not because you love God.

                    MILLS
Like, because someone's holding a gun on you.

Somerset stands, stretching, rolling his neck.

                    SOMERSET
No fingerprints.

                    MILLS
Nothing.

                    SOMERSET
Totally unrelated victims.

Mills nods, drinking from a beer.

No witnesses of any kind.

                    MILLS
Which I don't understand. He had to get back out.

                    SOMERSET
In any major city, minding your own business is a science. At crime prevention classes, the first thing they teach is that you should never cry 'help'. Always scream 'fire'. People don't answer to 'help', but 'fire', that's entertainment. They come running.

Somerset sits, turning his attention back to the photos.

He must have left another puzzle piece.

                    MILLS
Look, I appreciate being able to talk this out, but, uh . . .

SOMERSET

This is just to satisfy my curiosity. I'm still leaving at the end
of the week.

*Mills is very tired. He rubs his eyes, then walks to take one more photo
from his briefcase.*

*It is the photo of the framed picture of the falsely pretty woman with her
eyes circled in blood.*

MILLS

Gould's wife. She was out of town. If this means she saw
anything, I don't know what. We've questioned her at least
five times.

SOMERSET

And, if it's a threat.

MILLS

We put her in a safe house.

*Somerset nods. The SUBWAY TRAIN is HEARD RUMBLING
off-screen. The apartment begins to shake again, from the train passing
below. Mills runs his hands across his face, walks to the fridge to get
beer.*

*Somerset stays focused on the photo of the wife. His coffee cup rattles a
bit in its saucer and he reaches to steady it without looking. After a
moment, the RUMBLING LESSENS.*

Somerset runs his fingers over the eyes circled in blood.

Looking at the wife's photo.

SOMERSET
(*holds photo up*)

What if it's not that she's *seen* something? What if she's
supposed to see something, but she just hasn't been given a
chance to see it yet?

MILLS

Okay. But, what?

EXT. SAFE HOUSE – NIGHT

A grim motel with a broken neon and a promise of 'FREE HBO IN EVERY ROOM'. Somerset's car pulls up. Mills and Somerset get out, carrying file folders. They move to the entrance.

INT. SAFE HOUSE. HALLWAY – NIGHT

A poorly maintained elevator's door opens partially, then freezes up with a squeak. Mills squeezes out, followed by Somerset.

They head down the hall, where a POLICEMAN sits in a chair, bouncing a rubber ball off the floor and the wall and catching it. The policeman looks up at the detectives, doesn't seem to care who they are. Mills shows his badge.

MILLS
We're here to talk to Mrs Gould.

The policeman picks up a clipboard and hands it to Mills. Mills signs in. Somerset goes to knock on the room's door.

SOMERSET
(*to the door*)

Mrs Gould?

No reply. Somerset knocks a bit louder, opens the door a crack. He enters, clearing his throat.

SOMERSET
Excuse me . . . Mrs Gould.

Mills comes to enter with Somerset, shuts the door.

INT. SAFE HOUSE – NIGHT

Bad room. Plain, with water-spotted walls. Mills stands beside the woman from the picture, MRS GOULD, and shows her photos from the murder scene. The photos have been covered in sections to hide Mr Gould's corpse. Mrs Gould is crying.

Somerset is on the other side of the room, holding more photos.

MILLS
I'm sorry about this. I really am.

MRS GOULD

I . . . I don't understand.

Mills helps her flip through the photos. He isn't too keen to put her through this. Every once and a while, you can HEAR the KLUNK, KLUNK of the policeman bouncing his ball in the hall.

MILLS

I need you to look at each one carefully . . . very carefully. Look for anything that seems strange or out of place. Anything at all.

MRS GOULD

I don't know why . . . why now?

MILLS

Please, I need you to help me if we're going to get who did this.

Mrs Gould sobs quietly, wipes her tears.

Anything . . . anything missing or different.

MRS GOULD

I don't see anything.

MILLS

Are you absolutely certain?

MRS GOULD

I can't do this now . . . please.

Mills looks to Somerset, looks at the photos Somerset holds.

MILLS

Maybe we better wait.

Somerset looks at the photos in his hand. These show Mr Gould's corpse in the chair, not covered in any way.

SOMERSET

It should be now. There may be something we're not seeing.

MRS GOULD

Wait. Here . . .

What is it?

Mrs Gould points at the modern art painting on the wall in one photo. The painting is just splattered paint, abstract.

MRS GOULD

This painting . . .

MILLS

What?

MRS GOULD

Why is this painting hanging upside-down?

Mills turns to look to Somerset.

INT. LAW OFFICE – NIGHT

Where the greed murder took place. Somerset, wearing gloves, reaches to take the modern art painting off the wall. Mills is near, watching.

SOMERSET

You're sure your men didn't move this?

MILLS

Even if they did, those photos were taken before forensics.

Nothing on the wall behind the painting. Blank space.

Nothing.

SOMERSET

It's got to be.

Somerset puts the painting down, resting it on its bottom edge. The painting is backed by a thick sheet of brown paper stapled into the wooden frame. Somerset points to where the wire's eye screws used to be screwed into the frame, and to where it has been rescrewed.

He changed the wire to rehang it.

Somerset takes out his switchblade. Mills is surprised.

MILLS

What the fuck is that?

SOMERSET

A switchblade.

Somerset cuts along the edge of the brown paper to get to the hollow space between it and the back of the canvas. He cuts out the entire sheet. Mills helps pull it away. Nothing. Empty. Mills looks at both sides of the paper, then tosses it away.

MILLS

Nothing. Damn it!

Somerset lays the painting face up on the floor. He pokes his finger on the painted surface. He brings the flat of his blade against the painting, tries to peel some of the paint.

The killer didn't paint the fucking thing. Give it up.

Somerset pushes the painting away, frustrated.

SOMERSET

There must be something.

MILLS

We're screwed. He's fucking with us.

Somerset backs away from the wall, staring at the space where the painting hung. There is only a nail. He turns, looking around the office, then crosses the room.

Mills puts his hands to his temple, furious, picks up a lamp and throws it to the floor, venting.

Motherfucker!

Across the room, Somerset falls to his knees and pulls open a forensics kit. He takes out a fingerprint brush, examining the bristles. Mills sees this.

What?

SOMERSET

Bear with me.

Somerset goes back to the wall where the painting was. He pulls over a chair, gets on it and starts brushing near the nail.

MILLS

Oh, yeah, sure. You got to be kidding?!

SOMERSET

Just wait!

Somerset brushes with a few wider strokes. He leans close, studies the powder residue. Leans closer still. Pause.

SOMERSET

Call the print lab.

INT. MILLS' APARTMENT. BEDROOM – NIGHT

Tracy is asleep, dressed, with the lights still on. She stirs, then awakens and sits up slowly.

She squints from the light, sweaty and uncomfortable. She looks around and listens. All she hears is traffic.

EXT. MILLS' APARTMENT. LIVING-ROOM – NIGHT

FROM OUTSIDE, looking into the apartment, we see Tracy come in from the bedroom. She sees Mills and Somerset are gone.

She comes to open a window, then moves to the kitchen area.

We're still LOOKING IN at her as she starts the dishes in the sink. The RUMBLING of the subway train is heard. The room begins to rattle, as before. The dogs are heard whining.

Tracy looks out into the living-room, ill at ease.

INT. LAW OFFICE – NIGHT

The Male Forensic from the gluttony murder scene is here. He has a magnifying glass which he's using to study a very clear fingerprint in black powder on the wall.

MALE FORENSIC

Oh, man . . .

MILLS
(*off-screen*)

Talk to me.

The Male Forensic bites his lip, still studying.

Mills and Somerset are watching the forensic who works off-screen.

> (*to Somerset*)
> Just, honestly . . . have you ever seen anything like this . . .
> been involved in anything like this?

> SOMERSET

No.

> MALE FORENSIC
> (*off-screen*)
> Well, I can tell you, boys . . .

The Forensic steps down from a stool. Behind him, where the painting once was, are fingerprints, clear and distinct. The prints have been left, one after the other, to form letters which form words: HELP ME.

> MALE FORENSIC
> . . . just by looking at the shape of the underloop on these,
> they are *not* the victim's fingerprints.

INT. PRECINCT HOUSE. PRINT LAB – NIGHT

Dark. A TECHNICIAN sits before an old computer. The computer's green screen shows enlarged fingerprint patterns being aligned, compared and then rejected: whir – click – whir – click – whir – click. Mills and Somerset watch, bathed in a green glow.

> MILLS

He just may be nuts enough.

> SOMERSET

It doesn't fit. He doesn't want us to help him stop.

> MILLS

Who the hell knows? There's plenty of freaks out there doing
dirty deeds they don't want to do. You know . . . little voices
tell them bad things.

Somerset doesn't buy it. The Technician adjusts a knob, then turns to the detectives.

TECHNICIAN

I've seen this baby take as long as three days to make a match,
so you guys can go cross your fingers somewhere else.

INT. PRECINCT HOUSE. HALLWAY – NIGHT

*Somerset and Mills come out from the print lab. A janitor is mopping
the hall. The computer is HEARD WHIRing and CLICKing.
Somerset sits with a groan on a couch outside the lab door. Mills flops
beside him.*

SOMERSET

You meant what you said to Mrs Gould, didn't you? About
catching this guy. You really want to believe that, don't you?

MILLS

And you don't?

SOMERSET
(laughs, very tired)
I wish I still thought like you.

MILLS

Then, you tell me what you think we're doing.

SOMERSET

All we do is pick up the pieces. We take all the evidence, and
all the pictures and samples. We write everything down and
note what time things happened . . .

MILLS

That's all.

SOMERSET

We put it in a nice neat pile and file it away, on the slim
chance it's ever needed in a courtroom.
(pause)
It's like collecting diamonds on a desert island. You keep
them just in case you ever get rescued, but it's a pretty big
ocean out there.

MILLS

Bullshit.

SOMERSET

Even the most promising clues usually lead only to other
clues. I've seen so many corpses rolled away . . . unrevenged.

MILLS

I've seen the same. I'm not the country hick you seem to
think I am.

SOMERSET

If all the skeletons came out of all the closets . . . if every
hidden body were to suddenly rise again, there'd be no more
room for the living.

Somerset slumps back, takes out a cigarette and lights it.

MILLS

Don't tell me you didn't get that rush tonight . . . that
adrenalin, like we were getting somewhere.

Mills sits back on the couch, closes his eyes.

And, don't try to tell me it was because you found something
that might play well in a courtroom.

*Somerset looks at Mills, who crosses his arms to sleep. Somerset puffs the
cigarette. The computer is heard: whir – click – whir – click . . .*

INSERT – TITLE CARD: THURSDAY

INT. PRECINCT HOUSE. HALLWAY – EARLY MORNING

*Mills and Somerset are fast asleep on the couch, leaning against each
other. People pass and look at them strangely. A man steps in front of
the couch.*

He reaches with both hands to slap their faces simultaneously.

It's the Captain leaning over them.

CAPTAIN

Wake up, Glimmer Twins. We have a winner.

INT. PRECINCT HOUSE. HALLWAYS – EARLY MORNING

The Captain moves down the hall, passing photocopied mugshots over his shoulder to five hardened POLICE OFFICERS who follow, four men and one woman. The officers check their guns and secure bullet-proof vests with 'POLICE' spray-painted across them.

CAPTAIN

He goes by the name of Victor. His real name is Theodore Allen. His prints were found on scene by Homicide.

Somerset and Mills follow behind, drinking coffee, still waking up. The mugshots show a man, VICTOR, 25.

This guy has a long, long history of serious mental illness. His parents gave him a very strict, Southern Baptist upbringing, but somewhere along the line . . .

Two of the cops are talking.

You two can shut up now!

The two cops face front like huge, embarrased schoolchildren.

Thank you, fuckheads. Now, Victor dabbled in drugs, armed robbery and assault. Spent a couple of months in prison for the attempted rape of an under-aged boy, but his lawyer made sure he didn't stay. That lawyer was the recently deceased Eli Gould. The greed murder victim.

This news causes excited chatter among the cops.

We're finishing this today, ladies and germs. Victor's been out of circulation a while, but his residence is still in his name. A search warrant's being pushed through the courts as we speak.

They all round a corner. A red-headed cop, CALIFORNIA, leads the officers.

CALIFORNIA

So, have the housing cops walk up and ring the doorbell.

CAPTAIN

Listen, California. The media swarm's going to be there within forty-five minutes. If a shot's fired, they'll be there in ten. So, you better make good. I want headlines, not obituaries.

Mills looks to Somerset while the Captain continues the briefing.

MILLS

Does this do it for you?

SOMERSET

Doesn't seem like our man, does it?

MILLS

You tell me. I'm new in town.

SOMERSET

Our killer seems to have more purpose.

MILLS

The fingerprints.

SOMERSET

Yes. They were there . . . so, it must be.

MILLS

We'll tag along.

Somerset wants no part of that.

SOMERSET

Why would we?

MILLS
(*smiles*)

Satisfy our curiosity?

INT. MILLS' CAR – MORNING

Mills drives, follows a police van. Somerset rides shotgun. Mills seems pumped and ready. Somerset takes two Rolaids off a fresh roll and chews them.

MILLS

You ever take one?

Somerset takes out his gun, opens it to check the load.

SOMERSET

Never in my twenty-four years, knock on wood. I've only ever taken my gun out five times with the actual intention of using it. Never fired it though. Not once.

(closes his gun)

You?

SOMERSET... wait

MILLS

Never took a bullet. I pulled my gun once. Fired it once.

SOMERSET

And?

MILLS

It was my first one of these. We were a secondary unit. I was pretty shaky going in. I was still a rookie.

Mills takes a corner, tires screeching.

We busted the door, looking for this junkie, right? The geek just opened fire. Another cop was hit in the arm and he went flying . . . like in slow motion.
(pause)
I remember riding in the ambulance. His arm was like Jello. A piece of meat. He bled to death right there.

A pause.

SOMERSET

How did it end?

MILLS

I got him. I got that son-of-a-bitch. I was doing really good up till then. Lots of street busts. I've always had this weird luck . . . everything always went my way, but this was wild.
(pause)
I got him with one shot . . . right between the eyes. Next thing I know, the mayor's pinning a medal on me. Picture in the paper, whole nine yards.

Somerset unrolls the window, feels the air across his face.

SOMERSET

How was it?

MILLS

I expected it to be bad, you know. I took a human life . . . but I slept like a baby that night. I never gave it a second thought.

64

SOMERSET

I think Hemingway wrote somewhere . . . I can't remember
where, but he wrote that in order to live in a place like this,
you have to have the ability to kill. I think he meant you truly
must be able to do it, not just faking it, to survive.

MILLS

Sounds like he knew what he was talking about.

INT. SLUM BUILDING. STAIRWELL – MORNING

*The five cops from the briefing, fully geared up and ready, rifles and
handguns out, move quickly up the stairs in single file. Somerset and
Mills follow, guns out. Somerset is sweating bullets. Mills is wild-eyed,
juiced.*

*Crack vials and hypodermic needles on the stairs crunch under the cops'
heavy boots.*

INT. SLUM HALLWAY – MORNING

*The cops enter the dank hall. They move cautiously. A man is lying on
the floor, looking up, helpless, with dead eyes.*

*A door opens and a woman peeks out. The female cop points her gun
and the door slams. California, leading the group, steps up to apartment
303. He has a search warrant Scotch-taped to the front of his bullet-
proof vest.*

CALIFORNIA
(*to Black Cop*)

This is it. Give it up.

*The Black Cop hoists a heavy battering ram to California. The other
cops get on both sides of the door. Somerset and Mills hang back a few
feet, watching their backs.*

BLACK COP
(*points to Mills*)

Cops go before Dicks.

Many people are sticking their heads out of doors in the hall.

CALIFORNIA

Police! Open the door!!

California brings the ram forward with a splintering thud – once – twice – the door flies open. The cops storm in.

INT. SLUM APARTMENT. MAIN ROOM – MORNING

The apartment is incredibly dusty. The cops charge down the short hall into this room where a bed sits against the far wall. California moves up to the bed. Someone lies under the sheets. Three other cops move, all training their weapon on the bed.

CALIFORNIA

Good morning, sweetheart!

A blond cop goes into another room. California moves closer to the bed, gun up.

Get up, now, motherfucker! *Now!*

INT. SLUM APARTMENT ADJOINING ROOM – MORNING

The blond cop enters, gun trained, looks around in confusion.

The room's tables, chairs and floor are covered with hundreds of colorful, plastic air fresheners.

INT. SLUM APARTMENT. MAIN ROOM – MORNING

Mills and Somerset enter. Somerset looks at the cops around the bed, then looks at a nearby wall. His mouth drops in horror. On the wall, written in excrement: SLOTH.

SOMERSET

Jesus . . .

California kicks the bed, enraged.

CALIFORNIA

I said get up, sleepyhead!

He pulls the sheets off the bed and reveals the shriveled, sore-covered form of a man who is blindfolded and tied to the bed with a thin wire which has been wrapped time and time again around the mattress and

66

bed frame. Tubes run out from a stained loincloth around the man's waist and snake under the bed.

Fuck me!

Mills pushes past the other cops.

MILLS

Holy shit.

The cops recoil from the stench. Somerset steps up, putting his gun away.

SOMERSET

Victor?

BLACK COP

What the hell . . .?

CALIFORNIA
(to Somerset)
Check this out, Dick . . .

California points with his gun to the end of the man's right arm. The hand is gone, severed at the wrist long ago.

MILLS

It is Victor.

SOMERSET
(points to a cop)
Call an ambulance.

The blond cop enters from the other room.

BLOND COP

What the fuck is this?

CALIFORNIA
Somebody call a hearse, more like.

The female cop has gone to one wall where a sheet is pinned up. She pulls the sheet down. Pinned behind the sheet are fifty-two Polaroid pictures; all pictures of Victor tied to the bed, with a date written at the bottom of each picture. It is a visual history of Victor's physical decay.

What is going on?

Mills sees the female cop looking at the pictures.

MILLS
Hey, California, get your people out.

Somerset takes out rubber gloves and puts them on.

CALIFORNIA
You heard him. Hit the hall, and don't touch anything.

Somerset replaces the sheet over Victor, but not over his head.

The cops file out and Mills goes to examine the pictures. California stays by the bed with Somerset.

It looks like he's some kind of friggin' wax sculpture or something.

Somerset places his finger along Victor's throat.

MILLS
Somerset, you . . . you better look here.

Mills looks at the photos in awe. Somerset joins him.

MILLS
All pictures of Victor tied to the bed.
(*crouches, points*)
The last one is dated three days ago.

Somerset looks at the first photo. In it, Victor is bound and gagged, but he is healthy.

SOMERSET
The first one . . . it's dated one year ago. To the day.

Somerset wipes his sweaty face.

California stands by the body, behind Somerset and Mills. He lifts the sheet on the bed to look under it.

CALIFORNIA
Mother . . .

Mills kneels and lifts the sheet which had covered the pictures off the floor. There is an open shoebox underneath.

MILLS

What . . .?

On the side of the box: TO THE WORLD, FROM ME.

California leans close to Victor's gaunt, blindfolded face, examining with morbid curiosity.

CALIFORNIA

You got what you deserved, Victor.

Somerset leans down beside Mills. Mills looks through the shoebox. Inside are plastic, zip-lock bags. One contains small clumps of hair. One contains a yellow liquid . . .

MILLS
(*looking at bags*)

A urine sample, hair sample . . . stool sample. Finger nails . . .
(*looks to Somerset*)

He's laughing at us.

California is still close to Victor's face, when suddenly Victor's lips twist open and Victor lets out a loud, guttural bark.

California jerks back, shouting in fear, falling over a chair to the floor.

Mills and Somerset reel. They see California on the ground, scared out of his mind, pointing.

CALIFORNIA

He's alive!

Somerset and Mills look towards the bed.

Victor's lips move feebly as he lets out a sick, gurgling moan.

He's still alive!!

EXT. SLUM APARTMENT BUILDING – MORNING

A crowd has gathered at the entrance. Mills' car, the police van and two ambulances are parked on the sidewalk.

INT. SLUM HALLWAY — MORNING

The cops are in the hall holding neighbors at bay.

INT. SLUM APARTMENT. MAIN ROOM — MORNING

Three ambulance attendants are at the bed, working on Victor. One attendant uses wire cutters to clip through Victor's bonds.

INT. SLUM STAIRWELL — MORNING

Mills and Somerset are standing in the middle of one flight of stairs. Both are highly agitated.

                    SOMERSET
The way this has gone till now, I wouldn't have thought it was possible, but we may have underestimated this guy.

                    MILLS
I want him bad. I don't just want to catch him anymore. I want to hurt him.

                    SOMERSET
Listen to me. He's all about playing games.

                    MILLS
No kidding! No fucking kidding!

                    SOMERSET
We have to divorce ourselves from emotions here. No matter how hard it is, we have to stay focused on the details.

                    MILLS
I don't know about you, but I feed off my emotions.

                    SOMERSET
He'll string us along all the way if we're not careful.

Mills is looking at the floor, still burning. Somerset grabs him by the jacket.

Are you listening to me?

Mills pushes Somerset's hand off.

MILLS

I hear you.

There is a sudden, brilliant FLASH of LIGHT and the SOUND of a CAMERA ADVANCING. Mills and Somerset look.

Down the stairs, a Reporter has his camera up, pointed at them.

REPORTER

Say cheese.

He takes another picture, flashbulb flashing.

Mills goes down the stairs, grabs the reporter, a balding, almost silly-looking man with thick glasses and wrinkled clothing.

MILLS

What the fuck are you doing here?

The Reporter squirms, holds up a laminated press pass on a cord around his neck.

REPORTER

I have a right, officer. I . . .

Mills shoves him, and the Reporter stumbles a few steps, then falls to the landing below with a thud.

MILLS

That doesn't mean anything! This is a closed crime scene!

Somerset comes to pull Mills back. The shaken Reporter stands uneasily.

REPORTER

You can't do this! You can't . . .

MILLS

Get the fuck out of here!

The Reporter scrambles down the next flight, out of sight.

REPORTER
(off-screen)

The public has a right to know!

Somerset yanks Mills back harder, till Mills sits on the stairs.

How do those cockroaches get here so quick?

SOMERSET
They pay cops for the inside scoop, and they pay well.

MILLS
(*calming*)
Sorry about that . . . I just . . .

SOMERSET
(*sarcastic*)
Oh, it's alright.

Somerset starts back up the stairs.

It's always impressive to see a man feeding off his emotions.

INT. HOSPITAL ROOM – DAY

*Somerset and Mills are with DOCTOR BEARDSLEY. Victor lies
inside an oxygen tent with tubes running into him. The room is dim.*

DOCTOR
A year of immobility seems about right, judging by the
deterioration of the muscles and the spine. Blood tests show a
whole smorgasbord of drugs in his system; from crack to
heroin . . . even an antibiotic which must have been
administered to keep the bed sores from infecting.

Mills looks into the oxygen tent.

MILLS
He hasn't said anything, or tried to express himself in any
way?

DOCTOR
Even if his brain were not mush, which it is . . . he chewed off
his own tongue long ago.

Mills winces, moves away from the bed.

SOMERSET
There's no way he'll survive?

Detective, he'd die right now of shock if you were to shine a flashlight in his eyes.

Silence for a moment, then the Doctor lets out a chuckle.

It's funny to think . . . he's experienced about as much pain and suffering as anyone I've encountered – give or take – and he still has hell to look forward to.

He chuckles again, engrossed in some information on a clipboard. Mills looks to Somerset.

MILLS

Harsh.

INT. PRECINCT HOUSE. READY ROOM – DAY

A blackboard. Written in chalk, in large letters:

1	~~gluttony~~	5	wrath
2	~~greed~~	6	pride
3	~~sloth~~	7	lust
4	envy		

This case has taken larger quarters. What looks like a classroom with chalkboards on the walls and a podium at front has been converted to office space. Many desks and folding chairs. Only a few occupied. Much info taped up on the walls. Somerset and Mills are at their paperwork-covered desks near a window.

SOMERSET
(reading from one sheet)
Victor's landlord says an envelope of cash was in the office mailbox each month. He says, quote, 'I never heard a single complaint from the tenant in apartment three-o-one, and nobody every complained about him. He's the best tenant I've ever had.'

MILLS
A landlord's dream tenant: a paralysed man with no tongue.

SOMERSET
Who pays the rent on time.

Somerset turns to the typewriter, types. Mills fills out a form by hand.
He makes an error and tries to erase, but the paper rips. He curses,
crumples the paper and throws it.

MILLS

I'm sick of sitting around waiting.

SOMERSET

This is the job.

MILLS

There must be something in this pile of garbage we can
follow. I mean, Christ . . . do we have to let this lunatic make
all the moves.

SOMERSET

It's dismissive to call him a lunatic. Don't make that mistake.

MILLS

Oh, blah, blah, blah. The guy's insane. Right now he's
probably dancing around his room in a pair of his mommy's
panties, singing show tunes and rubbing himself with peanut
butter . . .

SOMERSET

No.

MILLS

Sooner or later his luck's going to run out.

SOMERSET

No. He's not depending on luck. You've seen that. We
walked into that apartment exactly one year after he first tied
Victor to the bed, to the day. To the day! Because he wanted
us to.

MILLS

We don't know for sure . . .

SOMERSET

Yes we do. Here . . .

Somerset picks up the photocopy of the first note.

This quote . . . his first words to us. It's from Milton's

74

Paradise Lost: 'Long is the way, and hard, that out of hell leads up to light . . .'

> MILLS

And so what?

> SOMERSET

Well, he's been right so far, hasn't he?

> MILLS

Just because the bastard has a library card, it doesn't make him Einstein.

> SOMERSET

Just, realize . . . the type of intestinal fortitude it must take . . . to keep a man bound for a full year. To connect tubes to his genitals. To sever his hand and use it to plant fingerprints. He's methodical and exacting, and worst of all, he's patient.

> MILLS

What does all that matter anyway? It's not our job to figure him out, is it? It's our job to catch him.

Something clicks for Somerset. He looks away, thinking.

Mills watches him.

What?

Somerset sits. Ponders, staring off into space.

What is it?

Somerset stands back up, takes money out of his pockets.

> SOMERSET

How much money do you have?

> MILLS

I don't know . . . like fifty.

Somerset picks up the phone and dials, still sifting through his own money. Mills doesn't know what's going on.

SOMERSET
(*to Mills*)

I propose a field trip.

INT. PUBLIC LIBRARY – DAY

Somerset walks through the busy main library, goes to a group of computer terminals. Mills follows, wound up. Somerset sits at one computer and works the keyboard, hunt-and-peck.

MILLS

Somerset . . . what the fuck?

Several people turn to shush him. Somerset takes out a notepad.

SOMERSET

At the top of the list, we'll put Purgatory, Canterbury Tales . . . anything relating to the seven deadly sins. Now, what the killer might research. What would he need to study to do the things he's done? What are his other interests? For example . . .

INSERT – COMPUTER SCREEN

Somerset types. On the screen: SEARCH: JACK THE RIPPER.

EXT. HOT DOG WORLD – DAY

The restaurant's sign reads: HOT DOG WORLD, HOME OF THE WORLD'S BIGGEST DOGS. A MAN is trying to give out paper advertisements. People walk out of their way to avoid him.

MAN
(*to people*)

Take one, you stupid fucks! Here . . . take one! It's a fucking coupon! Take it!

INT. HOT DOG WORLD – DAY

Mills and Somerset are in a booth, both on the same seat on the same side of the table. They look over their list of books. Mills goes to eat a hot dog, but Somerset stops him.

                    SOMERSET

They had about fifty health violations during the last
inspection.

Mills throws the dog down, looks at his watch.

                     MILLS

Could you at least sit across from me? I don't want people to
think we're dating.

*Somerset watches a GREASY MAN, wearing a black suit, enter. The
man's hair is slicked back.*

                    SOMERSET

Give me your money.

Mills hands his money to Somerset.

                     MILLS

I'm handing you this, and for some strange reason, I have the
idea I should know what the fuck we're doing.

*Somerset folds the money with his own into the list of books. He holds
the list in his lap, under the table. Greasy Man comes to sit at the table.*

                   GREASY MAN

Hey, Somerset. How are you? I didn't know this was going to
be a *ménage à trois*.

                    SOMERSET

It's not a problem.

                   GREASY MAN

Only for you do I do this. Big risk here . . . so I figure we'll be
even-up. All fair and square.

*Greasy Man has his hands under the table. He gets up to leave with his
hand in his pocket. He picks up Mills' dog.*

About an hour.

Greasy Man leaves, eating the hot dog.

                     MILLS

Well, that was money well spent.

SOMERSET

Let's go.

INT. PIZZA PARLOR – DAY

Mills and Somerset sit with a pizza before them.

SOMERSET

By telling you this, I'm trusting you more than I trust most people.

MILLS

It'd be best if you got to the point, 'cause I'm about ready to punch you in the face.

Somerset leans closer to Mills, speaks quietly.

SOMERSET

It's probably nothing, but even if it is, it's no skin off our teeth. The man at Hot Dog World is a friend, in the Bureau.

MILLS

Him?

SOMERSET

For a long time, the FBI's been hooked into the library system, keeping accurate records.

MILLS

What? Assessing fines?

SOMERSET

They monitor reading habits. Not every book, but certain ones are flagged. Books about . . . let's say, how to build a nuclear bomb, or maybe *Mein Kampf*. Whoever takes out a flagged book has their library records fed to the FBI from then on.

MILLS

You got to be kidding.

SOMERSET

Flagged books cover every topic the Bureau deems questionable . . . communism to violent crime.

78

How is this legal?

SOMERSET

Legal . . . illegal. These terms don't apply. I don't applaud it.

Somerset takes a bite of pizza.

They can't use the information directly, but it's a useful
guide. It might sound silly, but you can't get a library card
without ID and a current phone bill.

Mills is starting to warm to it.

MILLS

So they run our list.

SOMERSET

If you want to know who's been reading *Paradise Lost,
Purgatory,* and say . . . *The Life and Time of Charlie Manson,*
the Bureau's computer will tell you. It might give us a name.

MILLS

Yeah. Some college student who's taking English 101 and just
happens to be writing a paper on twentieth-century crime.

SOMERSET

Yeah, well . . . at least we're out of the office. We've got
pizza.

MILLS

How do you know all about this?

SOMERSET

I don't. Neither do you.

Somerset looks up. Greasy Man is entering the pizza parlor.

INT. SOMERSET'S CAR – EARLY EVENING

*Dusk. The car is parked with Somerset at the wheel and Mills beside.
They look through pages of connected computer paper.*

MILLS

This is a waste of time.

SOMERSET

We're focusing.

MILLS

I know, I know . . . focusing on one little thing.

SOMERSET
(*reading aloud*)
The Divine Comedy. A History of Catholicism. A book called
Murderers and Madmen.

He hands the sheets to Mills. Mills looks them over.

MILLS
(*reading*)
*Modern Homicide Investigation. In Cold Blood. Of Human
Bondage.* Human Bondage?

SOMERSET

It's not what you think it is.

MILLS
(*reads*)
The Marquis de Sade and Origins of Sadism.

SOMERSET

That is.

MILLS
(*reads*)
The Writings of Saint Thomas Aqu . . . Aquin . . .

SOMERSET

Saint Thomas Aquinas.
(*starts the car*)
He wrote about the seven deadly sins.

INT. TENEMENT BUILDING. STAIRWELL/HALLWAY – EARLY
EVENING

*Somerset and Mills walk up the stairs and turn a corner into a long
hall. Somerset is looking at the computer sheets.*

MILLS

You're sure you're reading that right? John Doe?

SOMERSET

That's what it says. Jonathan Doe.

MILLS

This is stupid. It'd be just too easy.

SOMERSET

We'll take a look at him. Talk to him.

MILLS

Sure. Uh, excuse me . . . are you by any chance a serial killer?
Oh, you are? Well, come with us then, if it's okay.

They reach a door, apartment 6A. Somerset knocks.

What are you going to say?

SOMERSET

You do the talking. Put that old silver tongue of yours to
work.

MILLS

Who told you about my silver tongue? You been talking to my
wife?

Mills knocks on the door, hard.

This is really lame.

A CREAK is HEARD off-screen. Somerset turns to look towards it . . .

*A male figure, JOHN DOE, is standing at the stairwell, wearing a hat
and standing in shadow, looking towards them. Stark still.*

Somerset furrows his brow.

Then John Doe reaches into his coat, lifts his arm, pointing . . .

SOMERSET

Mills . . .!

*BLAM – GUNFIRE SOUNDS, deafening, as a bullet slams into door
6A, just missing Somerset as he and Mills hit the floor.*

John Doe fires again . . .

The bullet blows a huge hole in the wall, throwing plaster. A third bullet follows, just above Mills and Somerset, and John Doe is heard running back down the stairs.

The gunfire's still echoing, ringing, as Mills gets up and unholsters his gun.

MILLS

Jesus Christ . . .

Mills scrambles to the stairwell . . .

IN THE STAIRWELL Mills bounds downstairs, turns a corner and leaps down another flight. He halts on the landing, listening. John Doe can be heard still running, below.

IN THE HALL above Somerset rolls and takes out his gun. He stands, dazed.

MILLS
(*off-screen, from in stairwell*)
What kind of gun was it?

Somerset comes into the stairwell.

MILLS
(*off-screen, from below*)
Damn it, Somerset . . . what kind of gun?! How many bullets?

BELOW, IN THE STAIRWELL, Mills hurries down more stairs.

SOMERSET
(*off-screen, from above*)
I don't know. Might've been a revolver.

Voices echo. Mills loses his footing, falls . . .

Mills hits the next landing hard, dropping his gun.

MILLS

Fuck!

Mills gets back up and picks up his gun and keeps going.

ABOVE, IN THE STAIRWELL, Somerset runs down the stairs, breathing hard.

> MILLS
> *(off-screen, from below)*
> What's he look like?

> SOMERSET
> Brown hat. Tan raincoat . . . like a . . . like a trench coat.

BELOW, IN THE STAIRWELL, Mills stops, gun ready. He moves to peer over the railing, down into the space at the stairwell's center . . .

John Doe is below, in shadow, aiming his gun straight up . . .

Mills jerks back as SHOT is FIRED from below and the bullet is heard WHIZZING . . .

Above, the railing near Somerset splinters into a million pieces, sends Somerset ducking for cover.

ANOTHER BLAST from below – the bullet is HEARD RICOCHETING above.

BELOW, Mills is crouched, waiting as the gunshot echoes.

> MILLS
> *(to himself)*
> Five . . . that's five . . .

He leaps up and continues down the stairs.

INT. TENEMENT BUILDING. LOWER HALLWAY – EARLY EVENING

Mills comes down the stairs and into a hallway, falling to one knee, sliding and pointing his gun one direction – empty hallway.

He wheels round to the other direction, gun hand shaking, and catches a GLIMPSE of John Doe just as he disappears around a corner far down the hall. Mills gets up, looking back to the number 2 by the stairs as he books, shouting back towards the stairwell . . .

> MILLS
> Second floor! Second floor!

Mills sprints, FOLLOWING him, tearing ass . . .

. . . AROUND THE CORNER. Mills makes the turn, full speed ahead, bringing his gun up . . .

Far ahead, John Doe's running . . .

Mills takes aim . . .

Ahead, between John Doe and Mills, a tenant in T-shirt and underwear comes out of an apartment, looking towards John Doe, blocking the line of fire . . .

MILLS

Get down! Move . . .!

The tenant turns to Mills, confused. Mills angrily pushes past . . .

Ahead, John Doe makes an abrupt halt. A woman tenant is looking out her door and John Doe grabs her and throws her into the hall. She falls as John Doe shoves his way into her apartment.

BACK AT THE STAIRWELL, Somerset comes down the stairs, tired. He runs.

AROUND THE CORNER, IN THE OTHER HALLWAY SECTION, Mills reaches the apartment Doe entered, bursting in . . .

INT. TENEMENT APARTMENT – EARLY EVENING

Mills enters, gun up. It's a railroad apartment, with all the rooms adjoining in a row. At the far end of the apartment, John Doe can be seen moving out one room's window on to a fire-escape just as that room's door is swinging shut.

Mills charges through the apartment, full on . . .

He bashes through the closed door . . .

EXT. TENEMENT BUILDING. FIRE-ESCAPE – EARLY EVENING

Mills leans out of the window over an alleyway. BLAM – GUNSHOT. The window above Mills shatters and he pulls back.

IN THE APARTMENT, Mills stays down for a brief second.

MILLS
(*to himself*)

Six! That's six . . .

He moves back to the window, just as BLAM, BLAM, BLAM – three more bullets rattle the window and window frame. Mills recoils.

Seven, eight, nine . . . Fuck!

OUT ON THE FIRE ESCAPE, Mills leans back out, slowly, searching, gun up.

Below, John Doe runs out the alleyway's mouth and rounds a corner, gone.

Mills scrambles out on to the fire-escape, running a few steps and then vaulting the rail . . . He crashes down on the roof of a car parked below. The windshield cracks.

Mills jumps off and continues the pursuit . . .

EXT. CITY STREET – EARLY EVENING

Mills rounds the alleyway corner into people-packed streets.

Several people are running, heading in several different directions.

Mills comes to a halt, his focus confused, searching desperately. Others run upon seeing his gun. Women scream and grab up their children. Mills can't see far down the sidewalk because of all the people. He moves forward . . .

He jumps atop a fire hydrant, gripping a street sign for balance, trying to see further down the street.

MILLS' POV: *There he is! John Doe can be seen, far off, moving across the street, through traffic, to the opposite sidewalk.*

ON THE STREET, Mills runs, into traffic, avoiding cars, down the center line. Angry drivers scream at him.

Ahead, John Doe glances back, ducking into an alley.

Mills gets to the other sidewalk, yelling for people to get out of the way . . .

EXT. CITY ALLEYWAY – EARLY EVENING

Mills comes to this tight alleyway. It's dark, with a long, tall, vertical sliver of street light far ahead. Mills runs . . .

Charging hard onwards . . .

A two-by-four swings out from a hidden nook along the side of the alleyway – slamming Mills in the face with a THWACK!!

Mills' gun hits the alley wall and clatters into a puddle.

Mills hits the dirt, on his back, nose broken and split, face bloodied. He cries out, rolling to his side, clutching his face.

The two-by-four is dropped. John Doe's feet cross a short distance. Doe's hand reaches to pick up Mills' gun. (We never see John Doe's face.)

Mills still lies on his side, stunned, spitting blood and cursing, when he feels the barrel of his gun against the side of his face. Mills freezes.

John Doe moves the gun slowly across Mills' face, till the barrel reaches Mills' mouth. The barrel is inserted between his lips.

The gun's hammer is pulled back.

Mills quakes, tries to open his eyes, but he's blinded by the blood from his broken nose. For an instant, there is a sudden, BRIGHT FLASH OF LIGHT.

After a long moment, the gun withdraws. From off-screen, the bullets fall out of Mills' gun on to his chest.

The gun is dropped. John Doe runs towards the sliver of light. He's gone.

Mills lies for a long moment, gasping. At the alley's entrance, Somerset appears.

SOMERSET

Mills . . .

Mills rolls, shaken, feeling to pick up his bullets and trying to rub the blood out of his eyes with his shirt sleeve. Somerset arrives.

Are you alright?

MILLS

I'm fine.

SOMERSET

What happened?

Mills gets up, collects his gun and pockets it, then walks past Somerset, heading back.

Mills . . .?

Mills starts running. Somerset runs to follow.

INT. TENEMENT BUILDING. STAIRWELL/HALLWAY – EVENING

Mills moves from the stairwell, driven, his nose still bleeding, heading for apartment 6A. Somerset takes Mills' arm, but Mills pulls away and keeps going.

SOMERSET

Wait . . . just wait.

MILLS

It was him.

SOMERSET

You can't go in there.

Somerset grabs Mills again and Mills shoves him off.

MILLS

The hell I can't! We get in there and we can stop him.

SOMERSET

We need a warrant.

MILLS

We have probable cause now.

Somerset grabs Mills and shoves him against the wall.

SOMERSET

Think about it . . .

MILLS

What the fuck is wrong with you?

Think about how we got here!

Somerset holds the computer paper, now crumpled in his hand. He waves it in Mills' face as Mills struggles.

We can't tell anyone about this. We can't tell them about the Bureau, so we have no reason for being here.

Mills stops struggling, breathing hard, seething, trembling.

MILLS
By the time we clear a warrant someone else is going to be dead.

SOMERSET
Think it through. If we leave a hole like this, we'll never prosecute. He'll walk.
> (*pause*)
We have to come up with some excuse for knocking on *this* door.

MILLS
Okay . . . okay . . . get off.

Somerset releases Mills. Mills looks around the hall, then goes right to door 6A and KICKS IT IN – the door jamb splinters and the door swings open to darkness for a moment before swinging back, half-shut.

SOMERSET
You stupid son of a . . .

MILLS
No point in arguing anymore . . .

Mills strides down the short end of the hall, towards a window.

> (*pointing back*)
Unless you can fix that.

Mills stops, looking out the window. It overlooks a weedy, overgrown courtyard where a THIN VAGRANT lies asleep on the concrete. Mills turns, looking back to Somerset.

How much money do we have left?

INT. TENEMENT BUILDING. STAIRWELL – NIGHT

On a stairwell landing, Somerset watches the Thin Vagrant from the courtyard talk to a uniformed POLICEMAN who writes on a clipboard, taking the statement.

> THIN VAGRANT
>
> So, I . . . I noticed this guy going out . . . going out a lot when those murders were happening. So . . . so I . . .

The Vagrant's clinging to the rail, drunk and out of it. Mills is down further on the stairs, high strung, chomping at the bit to get this over with.

> MILLS
>
> So, you called Detective Somerset, right?

> THIN VAGRANT
>
> Yeah, I . . . I called the detective. Because, because this guy seemed . . . creepy. And . . . and . . .

> MILLS
> *(urging him on)*
>
> And . . .

> THIN VAGRANT
>
> And, one of the murders was over there . . . over . . . nearby here. I . . . I called the cops . . .

The Vagrant wipes drool from his lips. Mills comes to grip him so he doesn't fall, searching the Policeman's face for suspicion.

> MILLS
>
> I told you the rest. You got it?

> POLICEMAN
> *(still writing)*
>
> Yeah, whatever.

> SOMERSET
>
> Have him sign it.

The Policeman holds the clipboard and pen out to the Vagrant. Mills takes the pen and guides the Vagrant's hand, almost signing it for him.

Great. Is that it?

The Policeman nods. Mills grips the Vagrant and leads him down the stairs in a hurry, around a bend. Mills looks up to be sure they're out of the policeman's sight, takes out a wad of cash and shoves it in the Vagrant's pocket.

Go drink yourself happy.

Mills quickly guides the Vagrant on his way, then turns and rushes up the stairs, taking them two at a time.

INT. JOHN DOE'S APARTMENT. MAIN ROOM – NIGHT

Mills pushes door 6A open, putting on rubber gloves. He steps in with Somerset behind. Somerset turns back to the Policeman.

SOMERSET
(*to Policeman*)

Wait outside.

Somerset closes the door most of the way. Mills hits a switch on the wall and a lamp illuminates a desk. The desk is in the center of the room, facing them. The room is bizarre, with some areas cluttered and others barren.

All the walls are painted black. All the large, curtainless windows are painted over.

Somerset puts on his gloves. Mills walks to the desk.

The desktop is rather tidy. The only blatantly strange thing is a set of notches carved into the wooden surface: three notches. A candle has been allowed to burn down at one corner of the desk and the wax trail goes all the way to the floor. Mills opens the middle desk drawer. It's empty except for the Holy Bible.

Somerset moves along shelves of books, looking at the spines. Lots of thick, oversized art volumes. A History of Theology. Handbook of Firearms. History of the World. Summa Theologica. United States Criminal Law Review.

At the desk, Mills opens another drawer. It's filled with at least forty empty aspirin bottles. He opens the next drawer and finds a rosary and several boxes of bullets.

Somerset comes to look at John Doe's 'bed'. No mattress. It's only a metal frame and springs with a sheet spread across it. The sheet is sweat-stained and dotted by stains of rust at many points where springs have worn through.

Somerset walks around the bed to a narrow table not far away against the wall. The table contains a strange tableau, like a mini stage, hand-made of cardboard and pasted Communion wafers. A human hand immersed in a jar of liquid is the centerpiece.

SOMERSET
(quiet, to himself)

Victor.

Above this, on the wall, there's a clutter of pinned-up articles about the seven deadly sins, pages from art books, pencil drawings of Christ, all tight together and overlapping.

Mills picks up a small piece of paper from a letter holder. It's a pink receipt from WILD BILL'S LEATHER SHOP. Written: CUSTOM JOB. *$502.64.* PAID IN FULL. *Mills puts the receipt back down on the desk.*

Somerset walks to a black door. Opens it.

INT. JOHN DOE'S APARTMENT. ROOM TWO – NIGHT

Somerset enters. A ceiling light is on. Bare bulb. There are bookshelves on three walls, filled with notebooks. Thousands and thousands of notebooks.

Somerset take one notebook down. It is a thick composition book with an unlabeled cover. Inside, the pages are filled with small handwritten sentences, thumb-nail sketches and blurry, glued-in photographs – small photos, seemingly cut from contact sheets. The sketches, pictures and writings take up every single inch.

Somerset takes down another notebook and flips through the pages. Same as the first, filled to the brim.

Somerset crosses to another shelf and pulls out another notebook. Same deal. Somerset looks around.

Jesus.

INT. JOHN DOE'S APARTMENT. MAIN ROOM – NIGHT

Mills moves from the desk to a hall. He tries a light switch, but it does nothing. He walks . . .

It's dark. A rather long hall. The only light is a red glow seeping from under the bottom of the closed door ahead.

INT. JOHN DOE'S APARTMENT. ROOM TWO – NIGHT

Somerset walks to a 16mm film projector. It sits facing a battered white screen. Somerset turns the projector on, backing away to switch off the bare bulc above.

INT. JOHN DOE'S APARTMENT. HALL – NIGHT

Mills reaches the door at the end of the hall. He turns the knob and pushes the door open. He's bathed in red light.

INT. JOHN DOE'S APARTMENT. BATHROOM – NIGHT

Mills enters. He looks around, slowly. Stunned.

INT. JOHN DOE'S APARTMENT. ROOM TWO – NIGHT

The projector is clattering in the dark, running a piece of film through. The film is spliced to run as a non-stop loop. Somerset watches the screen, light strobing across him.

The screen shows a bright image of clouds drifting, with strange superimposed angels in flowing robes floating jerkily. It's like a weird, old Hollywood version of Heaven.

The images switch abruptly to fire and tormented souls laboring around a pit of molten goo, where more tormented humans squirm. Like Heaven, it's a scratched piece of film from Hollywood's early days.

> MILLS
> (off-screen)

Somerset!

Somerset is engrossed in the images.

Somerset . . . come here!

Somerset hears him.

INT. JOHN DOE'S APARTMENT. HALL/BATHROOM – NIGHT

Somerset comes down the hall.

> MILLS
> *(off-screen)*

We had him, damn it.

Somerset reaches the bathroom where Mills stands looking up at the wall. The room has been converted into a dark-room lit by red bulbs with strips of film hanging from the ceiling.

> SOMERSET

What are you talking about?

> MILLS

We had him.

There are hundreds of prints on the walls and hanging from drying wires. Somerset looks around, trying to understand . . .

Pictures of John Doe's victims, alive and dead. Grotesque photos, of their pleading faces, and their dead bodies. Close shots of eyes, fingers and mouths.

Mills sits on the closed toilet, throwing something into the nearby sink and resting his head in his hands.

The pass was a fake.

In the sink – it's a laminated press pass on a neck cord.

On the walls, more pictures: of the crime scenes, but from the outside looking in. Long shots. Police cars. Ambulances. Uniformed officers putting up police barrier ribbons outside buildings. The coroner's wagon.

Somerset stares at them, taking them in, realizing . . .

We had him and we let him go.

*In the backgrounds of the pictures: Somerset and Mills. In another:
Mills crossing the street. In another: Somerset and Mills getting out of
Somerset's car.*

*One photo, close shot, shows <u>Mills and Somerset on the stairwell of the
building where Victor's body was found</u>. It is the picture taken by the
balding, almost silly-looking reporter.*

INT. JOHN DOE'S APARTMENT. MAIN ROOM – NIGHT

*A male forensic uses tongs to remove Victor's hand from the jar of liquid.
He places the hand in a clear plastic evidence bag.*

*The forensic walks away with the hand, past a FEMALE SKETCH
ARTIST who puts the finishing touches to an accurate drawing of the
balding, almost silly-looking reporter who wears thick glasses, now
known as John Doe.*

> SKETCH ARTIST
> You're sure this is him?

*Mills stands over the Sketch Artist. Two deputy detectives, SARA and
BILLY, are at work along with two other forensics searching,
photographing and dusting.*

> MILLS
> Just put it in circulation.

> SKETCH ARTIST
> You got it. Tomorrow morning, this city's good citizens will
> be on the lookout for Elmer Fudd.

> SARA
> *(approaching Mills)*
> We can't find anything to hang on to. No paystubs, no
> appointment books or calendars. Not even an address book.
> And, you're not going to believe this . . .

> MILLS
> Keep looking.

> SARA
> It's just . . . we haven't found any fingerprints yet. Not a
> single one.

94

You know, you're right, I don't believe you. Keep looking.

Mills walks away.

INT. JOHN DOE'S APARTMENT. ROOM TWO – NIGHT

Somerset and three uniformed officers are looking through the notebooks on the shelves. Somerset squints at the notebook in his hand, shaking his head as he reads. Mills enters.

Somerset looks up and closes the notebook.

SOMERSET

We could use about fifty more men here.

MILLS

I'm trying, alright? Just tell me what we've got.

Somerset pauses briefly at Mills' abruptness.

SOMERSET

Well, there are at least five thousand notebooks in this room, and near as I can tell, each notebook contains two hundred and fifty pages.

MILLS

Then, he must write about these murders.

SOMERSET
(opens notebook, reads)

'What sick, ridiculous, puppets we are, and what a gross, little stage we dance on. What fun we have, dancing and fucking, not a care in the world. Not knowing that we are nothing. We are not what was intended.'

Somerset turns a few pages.

(reads)

'On the subway today, a man came to me to start a conversation. He made small talk, this lonely man, talking about the weather and other things. I tried to be pleasant and accommodating, but my head began to hurt from his banality. I almost didn't notice it had happened, but I suddenly threw up all over him. He was not pleased, and I couldn't help laughing.'

Somerset closes the notebook.

No dates indicated, placed on the shelves in no discernible order. It's just his mind poured out on paper. I don't think it's going to give us any specifics.

MILLS

Looking around . . . I've got a bad feeling these murders are his life's work.

A PHONE is HEARD RINGING in another room. Mills looks.

INT. JOHN DOE'S APARTMENT. MAIN ROOM – NIGHT

Everyone's looking around, and at each other, trying to find the source of the RINGING. Mills and Somerset enter, baffled. Mills looks to Sara. She shrugs and shakes her head.

Everyone searches. PHONE RINGS.

Mills gets on his hands and knees.

MILLS

Here . . .

Mills crawls under John Doe's 'bed'. He comes back out with a rotary phone. Someone throws him a micro-cassette recorder. Mills turns the recorder on, makes sure it's running, then picks up the phone with the recorder to the earpiece.

MILLS
(into phone)

Hello.

JOHN DOE
(voice-over; from phone)

I admire you. I don't know how you found me, but imagine my surprise. I respect you detectives more every day.

MILLS
(into phone)

Okay, John, let's . . .

JOHN DOE
(voice-over; from phone)

No, no, no! You listen. I'll be back on schedule tomorrow,
even with this setback. I just had to call and express my
admiration. I'm sorry I had to hurt one of you, but I didn't
have a choice. You will accept my apology, won't you?

Mills says nothing, containing his anger.

I feel like saying more . . . but I don't want to ruin the
surprise.

John Doe hangs up. Mills puts down the phone.

INT. JOHN DOE'S APARTMENT. ROOM TWO – LATER – NIGHT

*Mills and Somerset stand in the dark, watching the continuous loop
projector's strange images of Heaven and Hell.*

MILLS

You were right.

Somerset looks at Mills.

He's preaching.

SOMERSET
(nods)

These murders are his sermon to all of us. To all us sinners.

*The door opens and light bursts in. The Captain stands there, looking
them over.*

CAPTAIN

It's been a long day, kids. Go home. Just make sure you sleep
with the phone between your legs.

INT. SOMERSET'S APARTMENT. BEDROOM – NIGHT

*Somerset winds his metronome. PHONE RINGS. Somerset does not
want to answer it, but does.*

SOMERSET
(into phone)

Hello.

TRACY
(voice-over; from phone)

Hello, William? It's Tracy.

SOMERSET
(into phone)

Tracy, is everything alright?

TRACY
(voice-over)

Yes, yes, everything's fine.

SOMERSET

Where's David?

TRACY
(voice-over)

He's in the shower, in the other room. I'm sorry to call like this.

SOMERSET

It's alright, I guess.

TRACY
(voice-over)

I, um . . . I need to talk to you. I need to talk to someone. Can you meet me somewhere . . . maybe tomorrow morning?

SOMERSET

I really don't understand.

TRACY
(voice-over)

I feel stupid, but you're the only person I know here. There's no one else . . .

SOMERSET

I just . . .

TRACY
(voice-over)

Can't you get away, for a little while?

SOMERSET

I don't know, with this case.

TRACY

If you can, please call me. Please. I have to go now . . .
goodnight.

Tracy hangs up. Somerset looks at the phone, wondering.

INSERT – TITLE CARD: FRIDAY

INT. COFFEE CAFE – MORNING

Somerset sits in the window booth with Tracy. The cafe is noisy. Tracy
stares into her coffee while she stirs it.

TRACY

I mean, you know this city. You've been here for so long.

SOMERSET

It's a hard place.

TRACY

I don't sleep very well.

Somerset is trying to be understanding, but sneaks a look at his watch.

SOMERSET

I feel strange being here with you . . . without David
knowing.

TRACY

I'm sorry, I only . . .

Two young punks step up to the window outside and look in at Tracy.
One flicks his tongue rapidly. Tracy looks away. Somerset takes out his
badge and holds it against the window. One punk gives the finger and
the other spits on the window. They leave, laughing. Tracy tries to
smile.

Perfect example.

SOMERSET

You have to put blinders on sometimes. Most times.

TRACY

I don't know why I asked you to come.

SOMERSET

Talk to him about it. He'll understand if you tell him how you feel.

TRACY

I can't be a burden, especially now. I know I'll get used to things. I guess I wanted to know what someone who's lived here thinks. Upstate, it was a completely different environment.
(*pause*)
I don't know if David told you, but I teach fifth grade, or did.

SOMERSET

He mentioned it.

Tracy seems very upset, near tears.

TRACY

I've been going to some of the schools, looking for work, but the conditions here are . . . horrible.

SOMERSET

You should look into private schools.

TRACY

I don't know . . .

Tracy looks up, wipes at her eyes.

SOMERSET

What's really bothering you?

Tracy bites her lip.

TRACY

David and I are . . . going to have a baby.

Somerset sits back, the expression of soothing concern on his face disappearing.

SOMERSET

Oh, Tracy . . . I have to tell you, I'm not the one to talk to about this.

I hate this city.

Somerset sighs. He takes out a cigarette, but thinks better of it and puts it back. He looks out the window.

SOMERSET

If you're thinking . . .
(*pause*)
I had a relationship once, very much like a marriage. And, she was going to have our child. This is a long time ago. She and I had decided we were going to make the choice together . . . whether to keep the baby.

Tracy looks at Somerset.

Well, I got up one morning and went to work . . . just like any other day, except it was my first since hearing about the baby. And, I . . . I felt this fear washing over me. I looked around, and I thought, how can I raise a child surrounded by all this? How can a child grow up here?
(*pause*)
So, I told her I didn't want us to have it, and over the next few weeks, I convinced her it was wrong. I mean . . . I wore her down, slowly . . .

TRACY

I want to have children. It's just . . .

SOMERSET

I can tell you now, I know . . . I'm positive I made the right decision. I'm positive. But, there's never a day that passes that I don't wish I had decided differently.

Somerset reaches and takes Tracy's hand.

If you . . . don't keep the baby, if that's what you decide, then, never tell him you were pregnant. I mean that. Never.
(*pause*)
The relationship will wither and die.

Tracy nods, tears welling up again. Somerset smiles a bit.

But, if you do decide to have the baby, then, at that very

moment, when you're absolutely sure, tell David. Tell him at that exact second, and then spoil that kid every chance you get.

There are tears in Somerset's eyes.

That's all the advice I can give you, Tracy. I don't even know you.

He smiles again, wipes his own tears.

TRACY

William . . .

Somerset's beeper begins BEEPING. He takes it out and stands, wanting to leave. Tracy gets up and kisses him on the cheek.

Thank you.

Somerset starts to back away.

Keep in touch after you're gone, William. Please.

Somerset nods, raises a hand to say goodbye as he leaves.

INT. WILD BILL'S LEATHER SHOP – DAY

Mills and Somerset are on one side of the counter and WILD BILL is on the other. Wild Bill is shirtless and covered in tattoos. He has a thick scar running down the center of his forehead and down his cheek. Leather belts, whips and jackets hang on the walls and from the ceiling.

WILD BILL

Yeah, he picked it up last night.

Wild Bill holds the pink receipt from John Doe's apartment.

MILLS

This was definitely him?

Mills points to the rendering of John Doe he holds.

WILD BILL

Yeah, John Doe. Easy name to remember.

What was this job you did for him?

WILD BILL
I got a picture of it here. It's a real sweet piece . . .

Wild Bill pulls a box from behind the counter, digs in it.

I figured he must be one of those performance artists. That's
what I figured. Like one of those guys who pisses in a cup on
stage and drinks it. Performance art.

Wild Bill hands a Polaroid picture to Mills. We do not see the picture yet.

MILLS
Oh . . . give me a break.

WILD BILL
I think I undercharged him.

SOMERSET
(*looks at photo*)
You built this for him? You built this?

WILD BILL
I've built weirder shit than that. So what?

A POLICEMAN enters the store.

POLICEMAN
Detectives . . . we have a situation.

Mills and Somerset follow the cop out.

WILD BILL
Hey, my picture . . .!

Wild Bill watches them go, scratches his thick scar.

Fucking pigs.

EXT. THE HOT HOUSE MASSAGE PARLOR – DAY

*It's a madhouse outside The Hot House, a bright red storefront bordered
on both sides by porno theater after porno theater. A crowd is gathered
around a police action in progress.*

Cops have formed a barrier, holding back the crowd and creating an aisle from the entrance of The Hot House to the back of a jail-van. Cops and detectives are escorting various men, women and transvestites into the large vehicle. The crowd, consisting of the dregs of society, is shouting. Some people are spitting and throwing trash at the cops.

INT. THE HOT HOUSE. RECEPTION AREA – DAY

TWO COPS are in front of a glass and steel cage. Inside the cage is a fat, BALD MAN with a wall of sex toys behind him.

                    BALD MAN
   Just wait! Just wait!

One Cop pounds his nightstick against the glass.

                      COP
   Get out of the fucking booth!

                    BALD MAN
   Just wait! I'll come out, just wait!

INT. THE HOT HOUSE. CORRIDORS – DAY

All the lights are red and the walls are painted red. Mills and Somerset follow a THIRD COP through the twisting corridors. POLICEMEN can be HEARD SHOUTING and MAKING ARRESTS. ROCK MUSIC PLAYS, throbbing. They come to a door.

                   THIRD COP
   I don't want to go in there again.

INT. RED ROOM – DAY

Mills and Somerset enter. ROCK MUSIC CONTINUES, LOUD. A strobe light flashes from the ceiling. TWO AMBULANCE ATTENDANTS are in the room. The First Attendant is placing a sheet over a bed, hiding the corpse of a blonde woman. The Second Attendant is trying to examine the pupils of a CRAZED MAN, 55, who is naked and wrapped in a sheet. A SWEATING COP holds the Crazed Man down.

CRAZED MAN
He . . . he . . . he made me do it!

SECOND ATTENDANT
I have to look at you. I have to look at you!

LUST *is scratched into the red paint on the wall in big letters.*

Mills and Somerset move towards the covered body.

FIRST ATTENDANT
(*to Mills and Somerset*)
You're not going to want to see this more than once.

CRAZED MAN
He had a gun! He made me do it!

The sheet is lifted for the detectives. They grimace at what they see. We do not see. Somerset closes his eyes and turns away. The First Attendant replaces the sheet.

Mills steps back, takes out his handkerchief and sucks on it. He looks at the Crazed Man. The Crazed Man jerks around while the Second Attendant preps a needle.

SECOND ATTENDANT
He's in shock, man. He's gone.

CRAZED MAN
Take this thing off me . . . take it off! Please, take this thing off me!

The Sweating Cop keeps his controlling grip on the crazed man.

Get it off . . . oh, God!

SWEATING COP
(*to Mills and Somerset*)
You're the detectives, right? Right? Well, you better see this!

Somerset's facing the wall. The Crazed Man's still yelling.

SWEATING COP
Hey . . . you better see what's strapped on to this guy!

Mills turns to the cop.

We've already seen it!

INT. SANATORIUM. WHITE ROOM – DAY

A Polaroid photograph on a white table. It is the photo Wild Bill gave to Mills. It's a picture of a belt, made with extra leather straps so it can be worn securely around the groin. It is a strap-on phallus, except there is no plastic protuberance. Instead, there is a metal knife – it's a strap-on butcher's knife.

CRAZED MAN

And . . . and . . . and he said . . . he asked me if I was married. And, I could see he had a gun in his hand.

SOMERSET

Where was the girl?

CRAZED MAN

What? What?

SOMERSET

Where was the prostitute? Where was she?

The Crazed Man leans forward in his chair.

CRAZED MAN

She was . . . she was on the bed. She was just sitting on the bed.

SOMERSET

Who tied her down? You or him?

CRAZED MAN

He had a gun. He had a gun . . . and he made it happen. He made me do it!
(*sobbing*)
He made me put that . . . that thing on. Oh, Christ! He made me wear it . . . and . . . and he told me to fuck her. He had the gun in my mouth.

The Crazed Man slides to the floor and hides his face in his hands.

The gun was in my throat!

Somerset looks up at the mirror in the room. He stands and picks up the Polaroid as two men in institutional uniforms enter to collect the Crazed Man from the floor.

INT. PRECINCT HOUSE. INTERROGATION ROOM – DAY

Mills stands in this dirty room with the dirty, Bald Man from The Hot House's reception area booth.

> MILLS
> You didn't hear any screams? Nothing? You didn't notice when this man walked in with a package under his arm?!

> BALD MAN
> No, I didn't.

> MILLS
> You didn't notice anything wrong? Nothing seemed strange to you?

> BALD MAN
> Everybody who goes in there has a package under his arm. Some guys are carrying suitcases full of stuff. And, screams? There're screams coming out of there every day. It goes with the territory, little boy!

> MILLS
> You like what you do for a living? You like the things you see?

The Bald Man smiles strangely.

> BALD MAN
> No. No, I don't. But, that's life.

INT. PRECINCT HOUSE. READY ROOM – EARLY EVENING

The blackboard:

1 ~~gluttony~~	5 wrath
2 ~~greed~~	6 pride
3 ~~sloth~~	7 ~~lust~~
4 envy	

The case has continued its growth. All the desks are now occupied. More information plastering the walls. Phones ring. Through a window into another room, one cop can be seen being interviewed by several eager reporters. Much activity.

Among all this, at their desks, Somerset and Mills are shell-shocked, silent. Somerset is looking at the blackboard. Mills is staring out an open window.

INT. SPORTS BAR – NIGHT

Somerset and Mills sit with a full pitcher of beer. The jukebox plays for the other customers. The walls of the bar are covered with trophies, plaques and other victory symbols.

> SOMERSET
> He'd come home and read me these morbid crime stories. *Murder in the Rue Morgue. Le Fanu's Green Tea.* My mother would give him hell because he was keeping me up till all hours.

> MILLS
> Sounds like a father who wanted his son to follow in his footsteps.

> SOMERSET
> One birthday he gave me this brand-new hardcover book, *The Century of the Detective*, by Jurgen Thorwald. It traced the history of deduction as a science, and it sealed my fate, because it was real, not fiction. That a drop of blood or a piece of hair could solve a crime . . . it was incredible to me.

Somerset drinks, then pours more beer. Pause.

> You know . . . there's not going to be a happy ending to this. It's not possible.

> MILLS
> If we get him, I'll be happy enough.

> SOMERSET
> No. Face it now. Stop thinking it's good versus evil.

> MILLS
> How can you say that? Especially after today?

SOMERSET

You tell me . . . a man has beaten his wife to death, or the
wife murdered the husband. Wash the blood off the walls. Put
the killer in jail. Who won?

MILLS

You do your job . . .

SOMERSET

Where's the victory?

MILLS

Follow the law and do the best you can. It's all there.

SOMERSET

If we caught John Doe and he were the devil, if he were
actually satan, that might live up to our expectations. But, this
is not the devil. It's just a man. There's not going to be any
satisfaction.

MILLS

Why don't you shut up for a while? You bitch and complain
. . . You think you're preparing me for hard times? You're
not. You quit, but I'm staying to fight.

SOMERSET

Who are you fighting for? People don't want a champion.
They just want to play lotto and eat cheeseburgers.

MILLS

Christ . . . how did you end up like this, huh? I mean,
seriously, if I thought like you, I'd have slit my wrists already.

SOMERSET

It wasn't one thing, if that's what you mean. It's just . . . I
can't live anymore where ignorance is embraced and nurtured
as if it were a virtue.

MILLS

And, you're so much better than everyone, right?

SOMERSET

Wrong. I sympathize completely. Because, in a place where
you can't win . . . apathy looks like a solution. Do you see? In

a lot of ways, it's easier to lose yourself in drugs than it is to cope with life. Easier to steal something than to earn it. Easier to beat a child than to raise it, because it takes *so much* work to love. Just as long as you never let yourself think about the abuse and the damage, or you risk being sad. Keep ignoring.

MILLS

You're talking about people who are mentally ill. You're . . .

SOMERSET

No, I'm not. I'm talking about common, everyday life here. If you want to survive, you can't afford to be this naïve.

MILLS

Fuck you. Fuck you! You say, 'The problem with people is they don't care, so I don't care about people.' It doesn't make any sense, and you know why . . .?

SOMERSET

But, you do care?

MILLS

Damn right.

SOMERSET

And you're going to make a difference?

MILLS
(*furious*)

Yeah, 'naïve' as that may sound. And, I don't think you quit because you believe the things you're saying. I think you want to believe them, because you quit. And, you want me to agree with you: 'Yeah, you're right, Somerset. This is a fucked place. Let's go live in a fucking log cabin.' Well, I don't agree with you. I can't. I'm staying.

Mills get up, throws some money on the table.

Thanks for the beer.

Mills leaves, other patrons watching him.

Somerset takes out a cigarette and goes to light it. The lighter will not light. When it finally does, Somerset's hand is trembling.

INT. MILLS' APARTMENT. BEDROOM – NIGHT

Mills comes quietly into the dark bedroom. Tracy is asleep on the bed. Mills takes off his suit jacket, puts it down.

He sits on a chair and unties one shoe, takes it off, then looks at Tracy. Looks at her a long moment.

He puts the shoe on the floor and goes to get on the bed. He kisses his wife's forehead, kisses her cheek, then wraps his arms under and around her. He holds her tight, kisses her again. Tracy stirs.

                    TRACY
      Honey?

Mills runs his fingers along her face.

                    MILLS
      I love you.

Mills holds her tighter. She wraps her arms around him. They lie together, clinging, holding tighter still.

INT. MILLS' APARTMENT BUILDING/STREET – NIGHT

Through the window of the apartment, we can see Tracy and Mills on the bed. CAMERA MOVES from this window, to the street.

CAMERA CONTINUES down the night street, to a car far from Mills' building. Inside the car, a MAN sits in darkness, silhouetted, looking up at Mills' window. He adjusts his thick glasses, sips from a coffee cup.

INT. SOMERSET'S APARTMENT. BEDROOM – NIGHT

Somerset is in bed. The metronome is sounding; tick . . . tick . . . tick . . . The SOUNDS of the CITY are LOUD.

Somerset closes his eyes, concentrating on the metronome. Tick . . . tick . . . tick . . . TWO MEN are HEARD from outside, YELLING at each other. Somerset rolls over, restless. Tick . . . tick . . . tick . . .

Glass is HEARD SHATTERING. Somerset opens his eyes. MORE GLASS, bottles being smashed. Somerset sits up. He reaches over, grabs the metronome and throws it against the wall.

INT. SOMERSET'S APARTMENT. LIVING-ROOM – LATER – NIGHT

THWACK. Somerset's switchblade hits the dartboard on the wall and the blade imbeds.

Somerset crosses the room, still dressed for bed. He is tense. He takes the switchblade from the dartboard, paces back across the room, turns, holds the blade, then throws. The blade sticks.

Somerset paces back to the dartboard, pulls the blade, paces back, throws the knife. THWACK. He goes to the board, gets the blade, paces, turns, throws. THWACK.

INSERT – TITLE CARD: SATURDAY

INT. JOHN DOE'S APARTMENT. MAIN ROOM – DAY

A clock on the wall says 12:30.

INT. JOHN DOE'S APARTMENT. ROOM TWO – DAY

Three deputy detectives are reading John Doe's notebooks. PHONE RINGS from the other room.

INT. JOHN DOE'S APARTMENT. MAIN ROOM – DAY

One deputy enters. He goes to the phone near the bed. The phone's been hooked into recording device with a speaker and tracing equipment. The deputy turns everything on, answers.

> JOHN DOE
> *(voice-over; through speaker)*
> I've gone and done it again.

INT. LUXURY APARTMENT. BATHROOM – DAY

Somerset is looking around this femininely decorated bathroom with a forensic, Gil. Both wear rubber gloves.

In the sink, objects covered in blood: a pair of scissors, a hypodermic needle, first-aid tape and gauze bandages, a bottle of anesthetic, a straight razor and a tube of Super Glue.

GIL

> He really did a number on her, didn't he?

Gil opens the plastic shower curtain and looks into the tub. The tub and shower wall are splattered with blood. The tub has a few inches of water in it. The water is cloudy red. A few bits of tape and gauze float in it. Gil jiggles the drain's knob. Some bubbles pop up from the clogged drain.

INT. LUXURY APARTMENT. BEDROOM – DAY

PRIDE *is written in lipstick on a full-length mirror. Below that:* I DID NOT KILL HER. SHE WAS GIVEN A CHOICE.

Mills and Dr O'Neill are in the room. O'Neill goes through his black bag. They're by a bed where a WOMAN lies dead under a blanket. The woman's head is sloppily bandaged with heavy white gauze and tape. The gauze is stained by spots of blood. Only her eyes and mouth have been left uncovered. A zoo's worth of stuffed animals have been placed across the bed. The woman holds a stuffed unicorn.

Somerset enters from the bathroom as Mills reaches to take the unicorn from the woman's grasp. There is a cordless phone in her left hand, and her hand clings to it.

Her right hand holds a bottle of prescription pills. Mills tries to open the fingers of this hand with a tongue depressor, but they are Super-Glued to the bottle. Mills turns the woman's hand slightly so two red pills roll out on to the blanket.

SOMERSET

> Sleeping pills.

Mills examines the left hand. The phone is glued into it.

O'Neill steps up, holding a thin pair of silver scissors. He leans to slide the scissors under the woman's bandage mask, starts cutting.

Somerset goes to a dresser where the woman's purse sits open. He takes out the driver's license and looks at the photo. The woman in the picture is stunningly beautiful.

> You see what he did?

Mills is watching the doctor work.

> MILLS
> He cut her up and dressed the wounds.

> SOMERSET
> *(holds up his left hand)*
> Call for help, and you'll live. But, you'll be disfigured.
> *(raises right hand)*
> Or, put yourself out of your misery.

O'Neill removes the bandages. Mills looks away. We do not see. O'Neill looks to the detectives.

> O'NEILL
> He cut off her nose to spite her face, and he did it very recently.

EXT. CITY STREET – DAY

Mills' car pulls up in front of the precinct house. Mills and Somerset get out. They wade through cars towards the old precinct house building.

> SOMERSET
> I've decided to stay on this, till it's over. Till it's either done or we can both see it's never going to finish.

Mills remains impassive.

> MILLS
> Oh, you want to stay now?

> SOMERSET
> One of two things will happen. We're either going to get John Doe, or he'll finish his series of seven, and this case will go on for years.

> MILLS
> You think you're doing me a big favor by staying?

> SOMERSET
> I'm requesting you keep me on as your partner a few more days. You'd be doing me the favor.

Mills walks on.

MILLS

You knew I'd say yes.

SOMERSET

No, actually, I wasn't sure at all.

Somerset and Mills climb the stairs of the precinct house. Behind them, in the street, John Doe's car pulls up and parks.

Cars behind begin BEEPING. People behind begin cursing and screaming for him to move.

John Doe steps out, his brown work boots, pants and shirt-tails splattered with blood.

He walks towards the precinct house, hands in his pockets, like he's out for a stroll. People on the sidewalk stop on seeing him, avoid him.

INT. PRECINCT HOUSE. RECEIVING LOBBY – DAY

Mills and Somerset walk past booking cubicles and benches of handcuffed low-lifes. Junkies are being led through by uniformed cops. The place is swimming with activity. The two detectives head to the wide duty desk at the end of the room.

SOMERSET

As soon as this is over, I'm gone.

MILLS

Big surprise.

They pass through a gate and Somerset goes towards a staircase leading upstairs. Mills stops at the duty desk. Other cops are vying for the DUTY SERGEANT'S attention.

Mills and Somerset are on the premises.

SERGEANT

Wonder-fucking-ful.

Another PLAIN-CLOTHES COP behind the duty desk leans over to hold out a few phone-message notes to Mills.

PLAIN-CLOTHES COP

Your wife called this morning. Do us a favor and get yourself an answering-machine, how 'bout it?

Mills nods and waves dismissively, pocketing the messages without looking at them and walking to follow Somerset.

JOHN DOE
(off-screen)

Detective.

Mills heads towards the stairs.

Detective!

Mills looks back . . . stops.

John Doe stands inside the precinct house doors. He gives a very slight smile.

I know you.

Somerset stops, looks back down the stairs.

Mills is staring at Doe, not comprehending.

Doe holds up his arms as if to say, 'Presto, here I am.' All eyes go to the blood-soaked figure of John Doe. There comes a sudden, near-silence in the room.

One UNIFORMED COP takes out his gun, points it at John Doe.

UNIFORMED COP

It's him!

Several other cops drop what they're doing and draw weapons.

Mills, still off balance, takes out his own gun, walking back through the gate. He points the gun at John Doe.

MILLS

Get down. Get down on the floor.

Cops move slowly in on Doe from all sides.

ANOTHER COP

You heard him, fuckface. Get down!

Somerset comes back through the gate.

Be careful!

John Doe gets down on his knees, hands in the air. Mills, pulse pounding, steps up, gun in both hands. Not too close.

MILLS
Down! Face on the floor!

ONE COP comes from behind and nudges Doe with his foot.

COP
Spread your legs and get your hands out in front of you!

John Doe lies on his stomach, obeying. Mills comes up and puts his gun right against Doe's head.

MILLS
Don't move. Don't move an inch.

ONE COP begins frisking Doe. Another comes to put on cuffs.

Somerset comes to Mills' side.

SOMERSET
I don't believe it.

JOHN DOE
(*to Somerset*)
Hello.

The Cop putting on the handcuffs looks up at Somerset and Mills.

COP
What the fuck is this . . .?

The Cop holds up Doe's cuffed hands. Doe winces. Every single one of Doe's fingers has a bandage wrapped around it.

John Doe tries to muster a smile, his face pressed against the floor, glasses askew, gun at his temple.

JOHN DOE
(*to Mills*)
I want to speak with my lawyer.

END OF ACT II

Mills holds a fingerprint card. The black ink prints are just useless blobs, smeared with blood.

Mills, Somerset and the Captain stand in darkness. Mills looks up from the print card through a two-way mirror into an interrogation room.

In the interrogation room, John Doe sits, handcuffed to the wall. This is not some superhuman serial killer.

He looks more like an eccentric college professor, not seething with anger, but looking round with calm, almost lazy eyes. The lawyer, MARK SWARR, sits taking notes and talking with Doe.

> CAPTAIN
>
> He cuts off the skin of his fingertips. That's why we can't find a single usable print in the apartment. He's been doing it for quite a while. Keeps cutting before the papillary line can grow back.

> MILLS
>
> What about the trace on his bank account and the guns? There must be something to connect him with a past.

> CAPTAIN
>
> So far it's all dead ends. No credit history. No employment history. His bank account's only five years old and it started as cash. We're even trying to trace his furniture, but for now all we know is he's independently wealthy, well-educated and totally insane. We may never know how he got that way.

> SOMERSET
>
> Because he is John Doe, by choice.

> MILLS
>
> When do we get to question him?

> CAPTAIN
>
> You don't. It goes to court now.

> MILLS
>
> He wouldn't just turn himself in. It doesn't make any sense.

Somerset moves from the window, crossing the room to sit.

CAPTAIN

Well, there he sits. It's not supposed to make sense.

SOMERSET

He's not finished.

MILLS

He's pissing in our faces again and we're just taking it.

CAPTAIN

You're wound too tight, Mills. Let it go.

The Captain walks. Mills is furious. He presses his fingers against the two-way mirror, pushes to crack his knuckles loudly.

MILLS
(*to Somerset*)

You know he's fucking us.

SOMERSET

You and I are, probably for the first time ever, in total agreement. He wouldn't just stop.

MILLS

Well . . . what the fuck, man?

SOMERSET

He's only two murders away from finishing his masterpiece, right? I can't even imagine how he'll try to finish it. Can you?

Mills looks in at John Doe. Somerset comes to stand beside him.

MILLS

No.

SOMERSET

We'll wait for his plea.

INT. PRECINCT HOUSE. READY ROOM – DAY

Mills is at the desk, feet up. He stares at the blackboard.

1	~~gluttony~~	5	wrath
2	~~greed~~	6	~~pride~~
3	~~sloth~~	7	~~lust~~
4	envy		

Clock on the wall says 4:45. Somerset packs books into boxes, preparing for his eventual departure. No one else is around.

The Captain opens the door, steps in and clears his throat, looking like there is something making him very unhappy.

INT. PRECINCT HOUSE. CAPTAIN'S OFFICE – DAY

Mills and Somerset stand together. The Captain is behind his desk with Martin Talbot, the DA, seated in front of him. Mark Swarr is addressing them all; he seems nervous but in control.

> SWARR
>
> My client says there are two more bodies . . . two more victims, hidden away. He will take Detectives Mills and Somerset to these bodies, but only Detectives Mills and Somerset. Only at six o'clock today.

Talbot wipes his moist brow with a handkerchief.

> TALBOT
>
> Oh, Christ.

> MILLS
>
> Why us?

> SWARR
>
> He says he admires you.

> SOMERSET
> *(to Captain)*
>
> This is all part of his game.

> SWARR
>
> My client claims that if the detectives do not accept this offer, these two bodies will never be found.

> CAPTAIN
>
> Frankly, counselor, I'm inclined to let them rot.

> TALBOT
>
> We don't make deals, Mr Swarr.

Mills gets in Swarr's face.

MILLS

How is it defending a scumbag like this? You proud of yourself?

CAPTAIN

Ease back, Mills.

SWARR

I'm required by law to serve my clients to the best of my ability, and to serve their best interests.

Mills backs off.

CAPTAIN

Well, we're going to have to pass.

SWARR

My client . . . he also wishes to inform you, if you do not accept, he will plead insanity, across the board.

TALBOT
(*to no one in particular*)
Let him try! I'd like to see him try!

SWARR

Come now, Martin. We all know, with the extreme nature of these crimes, I could get him off with such a plea.

Talbot considers this, wringing the handkerchief in his hands. Mills looks at Somerset. Somerset looks at him.

TALBOT

I'm not letting this conviction slide, I can tell you that right here and right now!

SWARR

He says, if you accept, under his specific conditions, he will sign a full confession and plead guilty . . . right here, right now.

Talbot glares at Swarr.

CAPTAIN
(*to Mills*)

What do you think?

MILLS

I'm in.

SWARR

It has to be both of you.

SOMERSET

If he were to claim insanity, this conversation is admissible. The fact that he's blackmailing us with his plea . . .

SWARR

And, my client reminds you, two more are dead. The press would have a field day if they found out the police didn't seem too concerned about finding them . . . giving them a proper burial.

SOMERSET

If there *really are* two more dead.

The Captain picks up a sheet from his desk.

CAPTAIN

The lab report came up from downtown. They did a quickie on Doe's clothing and fingernails. They found blood from Doe, from him cutting his own fingers . . . There was blood from the woman whose face he cut off, and blood from a third party. As yet unidentified.

TALBOT
(*to Somerset*)

You would be escorting an unarmed man.

Somerset thinks it over. He looks to Mills.

MILLS

Let's finish it.

Somerset looks at the floor, then at Swarr.

SOMERSET
(*to the Captain*)

Well . . . get the fucking lawyer out of the room and we can talk about how this whole thing's going to go down.

INT. PRECINCT HOUSE. BATHROOM/LOCKER ROOM – DAY

Somerset's hand reaches to the sink to pick up a razor.

Somerset and Mills are at the sinks, looking at themselves in mirrors, shirtless. They have shaving cream spread across their chests. Somerset flicks his cigarette in the sink, then brings the razor up to start shaving the hair off his chest. Mills is already doing the same.

                    SOMERSET
If John Doe's head splits open and a UFO flies out, I want
you to have expected it.

                    MILLS
I will.

They continue shaving.

If I were to accidentally cut off one of my nipples, would that
be covered by workman's compensation?

Somerset smiles just slightly.

                    SOMERSET
I suppose so.
                    (*pause*)
If you were man enough to actually file the claim, I'd buy you
a new one out of my own pocket.

Mills finishes shaving, washes and wipes his chest off with a towel. He turns dead serious.

                    MILLS
Listen, Somerset . . . I uh . . .

Mills pauses, sighs. Somerset stops shaving and looks at him.

                    SOMERSET
What is it?

                    MILLS
Well . . .
                    (*pause*)
It's nothing.

Mills continues shaving. Somerset watches him.

INT. PRECINCT HOUSE READY ROOM – DAY

Somerset and Mills have their shirts open. A female technician tapes a small radio transmitter and microphone to Mills' chest. Somerset is already wired up, pressing the adhesive to make sure it'll hold.

The technician finishes prepping Mills. Somerset buttons up his shirt. The technician packs up her kit, leaving. The room is quiet. Somerset picks up his bullet-proof vest, slides into it.

Mills looks at his watch. He puts on his own vest, fastening it tight. He looks at Somerset.

Somerset takes out a roll of Antacids and pops a few. Mills holds out his hand and waits for an Antacid. Somerset looks at him, flicks a few into Mills' palm. Mills chews them.

SOMERSET

Cold as ice.

Somerset picks up his gun off a chair. Mills picks up his gun. They both check them out and close them up. They lay the guns in the holsters at the small of their backs.

They look at each other. Somerset holds out his hand. Mills shakes it.

INT. CITY STREET. PRECINCT HOUSE FRONT – DAY

The street is full of shadows as the sun is falling low. At the front of the precinct house, a throng of reporters shifts anxiously. A line of policemen holds them back.

Martin Talbot steps out of the precinct house, cops on either side of him. The press swarm lurches forward, flashbulbs exploding. Talbot holds out his hands, preparing to speak.

EXT. CITY STREET. PRECINCT HOUSE REAR – DAY

At the rear of the precinct house, Somerset's car pulls out of the fenced-in parking lot. The car speeds up on the street and turns a corner, heading into the grim city.

EXT. SKYSCRAPER ROOFTOP – DAY

California is dressed in full battle gear, looking through binoculars to the city below. The wind blows hard.

A Pilot, holding two helmets, comes up behind California. A sleek police helicopter sits on the roof's helipad.

> CALIFORNIA
> Is this wind going to hurt us?

> PILOT
> Just makes the ride more fun.

The cocky Pilot grins.

INT. SOMERSET'S CAR – DAY

Somerset is at the wheel. Mills is in the passenger's seat, looking back at John Doe through protective wire mesh. Doe's in the back seat. His handcuffs are attached to ankle cuffs by a length of chain. He is dressed in gray pants and a gray shirt, looking out the window, sweaty but placid.

> SOMERSET
> Who are you, John? Who are you really?

John Doe looks to Somerset's eyes in the rear-view mirror.

> JOHN DOE
> What do you mean?

> SOMERSET
> I mean, at this point, what would it hurt if you told us a little about yourself?

> JOHN DOE
> (*pause*)
> It doesn't matter who I am. Who I am means absolutely nothing.
> (*looking out, to Somerset*)
> You need to turn left here . . . at the traffic lights.

> MILLS
> Where we headed?

JOHN DOE

You'll see.

Mills looks at Doe for a long time in silence.

MILLS

We're not just going to pick up two more bodies, are we, Johnny? That wouldn't be . . . shocking enough. Wouldn't keep you on the front page of the newspapers.

JOHN DOE

Wanting people to pay attention, you can't just tap them on the shoulder. You have to hit them in the head with a sledgehammer. Then, you have their strict attention.

MILLS

What makes you so special that people should pay attention?

JOHN DOE

Not me. I'm not special. I'm not exceptional.
(*pause*)
This is, though. What I'm doing.

MILLS

There's nothing unusual about these precious murders of yours.

JOHN DOE

You know that's not true.

MILLS

In two months, no one's going to even remember this happened.

Doe looks down for a moment, then looks up, almost shyly.

JOHN DOE

You can't see the whole . . . the whole complete act yet. Not yet. But, when this is done, it's going to be . . . so . . . so . . .

MILLS

Spit it out.

JOHN DOE

It's going to be flawless. People will barely comprehend, but they won't be able to deny it.

MILLS

Could you possibly be any more non-specific? I mean, as master plans go, yours is pretty damn nebulous.

Doe looks down, licking his lips. He clenches his hands into fists, digging his bandaged fingertips into his sweaty palms.

JOHN DOE

I can't wait for you to see. I can't wait . . .
                    (*pause, looks to Mills*)
It's really going to be something.

MILLS

Well, I'll be standing right beside you the whole time, so you be sure to let me know when this whole, complete reality thing is done. Wouldn't want to miss it.

JOHN DOE

Oh, don't worry. You won't . . .

INT. POLICE HELICOPTER – DAY

The helicopter is in flight above the city. California is strapped in, hanging out the door. He holds a high-powered automatic rifle, wears goggles and a helmet/headset.

JOHN DOE
                    (*voice-over; through headset*)
. . . you won't miss a thing.

The other armed cops sit in the belly of the chopper. California leans in and looks up towards the Pilot.

CALIFORNIA
                    (*into helmet microphone*)
Head over the bridge and keep them in sight. Just keep your distance.

The Pilot looks back and nods.

EXT. CITY SKY — DAY

The chopper dips, flying like a bullet over the polluted city, heading towards the setting sun.

EXT. CITY STREETS — DAY

Somerset's car moves along a highway at river's edge. Heading for a huge suspension bridge filled with speeding traffic ahead.

INT. SOMERSET'S CAR — DAY

John Doe has his head against the window, looking up at the bridge, excited. He sits back, glances out the back window, then faces front, bites his lip, fidgety, like a kid on Christmas Eve.

Somerset's watching him through the rear-view mirror.

> SOMERSET

What's so exciting?

> JOHN DOE

It's not too far away now.

> MILLS
> (*to John Doe*)

I've been wondering, and maybe you can shed some light on this for me. Does an insane person know he's insane? Like, here's what I mean . . . When you're in bed at night, and you're almost about to fall asleep, do you ever just stop and say to yourself, 'Man, oh, man, am I ever nuts. It's interesting, what a complete fucking fruitcake I am.' Does that happen? Huh?

> JOHN DOE

It's more comfortable for you . . . to label me insane.

> MILLS

Seems a pretty accurate label to me.

> JOHN DOE

It's something I wouldn't expect you to accept . . . but, I didn't choose this. I was chosen.

Sure you were.

SOMERSET

I don't have any doubt you believe that, John. But, you're ignoring a glaring contradiction there.

Silence. Doe lets a long moment pass, hesitant.

JOHN DOE

Meaning what?

SOMERSET

Well, I'm glad you asked. See, if you were chosen . . . as if by some higher power, and your hand was forced . . . well . . .

Somerset turns in his seat to look Doe in the eye.

. . . then it's strange you took so much pleasure in it.

Somerset stares at Doe. Doe stares back. After a moment, Somerset turns back to the road ahead.

You enjoyed torturing your victims. That's not really in keeping with your martyrdom, is it?

It's the first time anything's gotten to Doe. He's ashamed, though trying not to let it bother him.

JOHN DOE
(long pause)

I . . . I doubt I enjoyed it any more than . . . Detective Mills would enjoy some time alone with me in a room without windows.
(looks to Mills)
Isn't that true? How happy would it make you to hurt me, with impunity.

MILLS
(coy mocking)

Now . . . I wouldn't do something like that, Johnny. I like you. I like you a lot.

JOHN DOE

You wouldn't because you know there are consequences. It's

in those eyes of yours, though . . . nothing wrong with a man taking pleasure in his work.

(*pause, shakes his head*)

I won't deny my own personal desire to turn each sin against the sinner. I only took their sins to logical conclusions.

MILLS

You only killed a bunch of innocent people so you could get your rocks off. That's all.

JOHN DOE

Innocent? Is that supposed to be funny? Look at the people I killed. An obese man, a disgusting man who could barely stand up . . . who if you saw him on the street, you'd point so your friends could mock him along with you. Who if you saw him while you were eating, you wouldn't be able to finish your meal. After him I picked the lawyer. And, you both must have been secretly thanking me for that one. This was a man who dedicated his life to making money by lying with every breath he could muster . . . to keeping rapists and murderers on the streets.

MILLS

Murderers?

JOHN DOE
(*ignoring*)

A woman . . .

MILLS

Murderers like you?

JOHN DOE
(*ignoring, louder*)

A woman . . . so ugly on the inside that she couldn't bear to go on living if she couldn't be beautiful on the outside. A drug dealer . . . a drug-dealing pederast, actually.

(*laughs at that one*)

And, don't forget the disease-spreading whore. Only in a world this shitty could you even try to say these were innocent people and keep a straight face.

(*getting worked up*)

That's the point. You see a deadly sin on almost every street corner, and in every home, literally. And we tolerate it. Because it's common, it seems trivial, and we tolerate, all day long, morning, noon and night. Not anymore. I'm setting the example, and it's going to be puzzled over and studied and followed, from now on.

MILLS

Delusions of grandeur.

JOHN DOE

You should be thanking me.

MILLS

And, why is that?

JOHN DOE

You're going to be remembered, and it's all because of me. And, the only reason I'm here right now is because I wanted to be.

MILLS

We would have found you eventually.

JOHN DOE

Really? Just biding your time, then? Toying with me. Is that it? Letting five people die until you finally felt like springing your trap?

Doe sits forward, slowly getting to Mills.
(*angrily*)
Tell me what it was that gave me away. What was the piece of evidence you were going to use against me right before *I* walked up to *you* and put my hands in the air.

MILLS

I seem to remember us knocking on your door.

JOHN DOE

And, I remember breaking your nose.
(*leans further forward*)
You're only alive because I didn't kill you.

Sit back.

John Doe doesn't sit back, staying very close to the wire mesh.

JOHN DOE
I spared you, and you're going to have to remember that
every time you look in the mirror at that nose on your face for
the rest of your life. Or, I should say, for the rest of what life
I've allowed you to have.

Mills slams his fist against the mesh, fed up, furious.

MILLS
I said, sit back, freak. Sit back and shut your fucking mouth!

Doe sits back, taking a deep breath and letting it out.

*In the front seat, Somerset shoots a concerned glance at Mills, then looks
up into the rear-view mirror.*

IN THE MIRROR: Doe, calm, gives Somerset a smile.

*Doe then turns his attention back out the passenger window, watching
the world pass by, his face pressed on the glass.*

*Mills sits forward in his seat, letting his anger come down. Doe keeps
staring out the window. A long pause.*

JOHN DOE
Don't ask me to pity the people I killed. I don't mourn them
any more than I mourn the thousands who died in Sodom
and Gomorrah.

Mills almost lets this pass, but can't. Blunted anger:

MILLS
You fuck. You really think what you did was God's good
work?

*Pause. John Doe is pressing his forefinger into the tip of his thumb,
causing blood to drip from under the bandage.*

JOHN DOE
The Lord works in mysterious ways.

EXT. SKY – EARLY EVENING

The helicopter flies over huge, blackened industrial parks, past smokestacks spewing soot. The sky is turning crimson.

INT. POLICE HELICOPTER – EARLY EVENING

California leans way out, looking back at the city.

EXT. INDUSTRIAL ROAD – EARLY EVENING

Somerset's car comes down this rocky, deserted strip, towards the industrial parks. The car tosses dirt into the air where it is captured on the wind.

EXT. SKY – EARLY EVENING

The chopper roars, low, close to the stretch of the industrial road. This is the only road through vast swampy fields. The industrial parks are far behind.

INT. POLICE HELICOPTER – EARLY EVENING

California still leans out, gun poised, looking over the fields.

> **CALIFORNIA**
> There ain't no ambush out here. There ain't no fucking nothing out here.

> **PILOT**
> *(voice-over; through headset)*
> We got about two minutes before they come up behind us.

> **CALIFORNIA**
> Go high. Way up. In sixty seconds, cut to the west.

EXT. SKY – EARLY EVENING

The chopper climbs, really moving.

EXT. INDUSTRIAL ROAD – EARLY EVENING

Somerset's car comes down the road, surrounded by marshlands.

The car slows, then stops. Mills gets out and goes to extract Doe.

Somerset gets out, looking east to the industrial parks and city beyond. The sky is darkening.

Somerset walks and looks to the west. The sky is red. Very far away, a passenger train moves towards the hidden sun.

Somerset watches the train, walking to the edge of the roadway. He looks down and steps back from what he sees.

A dead dog lies in the weeds, old and moldering.

Somerset turns to the car, where John Doe stands with Mills. Doe points with his cuffed hands to the dog, grins.

> JOHN DOE
> I didn't do that.

EXT. MARSHLANDS – EARLY EVENING

The wind howls, pounding on John Doe as he walks through the swampy fields. He walks slowly, encumbered by the deep muck and by the short chain between his ankles. Mills is with Doe, disgusted by the ooze covering his shoes and pants cuffs. He looks ahead, cautious. Somerset walks behind them.

Doe keeps looking back towards the car on the industrial road.

> MILLS
> What are you looking for?

Doe looks forward.

> JOHN DOE
> What time is it?

> SOMERSET
> Why?

Somerset looks at his watch. It's one minute after seven.

> JOHN DOE
> I want to know.

Mills gives Doe a shove.

Somerset looks back towards the industrial road, worried.

> MILLS

Just keep leading the way.

> JOHN DOE

It's close.

> SOMERSET

Mills!

Mills and Doe look back at Somerset. Somerset is facing the industrial road, pointing. A van is coming, dust flying.

Somerset looks at Mills. Mills looks at Somerset. They take out their guns. Somerset starts towards the road.

Stay with him.

> MILLS

Wait!

> SOMERSET

There's no time to discuss it!

Somerset runs to head off the van.

John Doe begins walking to follow Somerset.

> JOHN DOE

There he goes.

Mills levels his gun at John Doe's head.

EXT. MARSHLANDS. NEAR INDUSTRIAL ROAD – EARLY EVENING

Somerset runs, breathing hard, opening the top of his bullet-proof vest to speak into his hidden microphone.

> SOMERSET

There's a van . . . coming down the industrial road. Coming from the east.

INT. POLICE HELICOPTER – EARLY EVENING

The chopper is circling in the air, far from the marshlands with the sun behind it. Another cop is in the hatchway beside California, looking through binoculars.

SOMERSET

(voice-over; through headset)

The van is coming from the east. I don't know what it is. Come around. Come around.

EXT. MARSHLANDS. NEAR INDUSTRIAL ROAD – EARLY EVENING

Somerset continues, charging through the mire.

SOMERSET

Just get ready for anything and wait for my signal. Wait for me.

EXT. MARSHLANDS – EARLY EVENING

Mills keeps the gun on John Doe; he watches Somerset far off.

JOHN DOE

It's good we have some time to talk.

Doe starts walking again.

MILLS

Get down. Get down on your knees!

Mills grabs Doe and pushes Doe's knees out with his foot, making Doe kneel in the brown water.

Mills positions himself behind Doe so that Doe is between him and the road. Now, Mills can keep the gun on Doe and still watch Somerset.

EXT. MARSHLANDS. INDUSTRIAL ROAD – EARLY EVENING

Somerset comes up on the road, near his car. He signals for the van to stop, then fires a warning shot in the air. The van is about one hundred yards away, still coming.

Somerset walks towards it, breathless, pointing his gun.

SOMERSET

Stop the van! Stop!

The van brakes, wheels sliding on the loose roadway. Stops. Somerset moves up to it, staying about ten feet away.

Get out! Get out with your hands on your head! Do it now!

The driver of the van, a DELIVERYMAN, pushes the door open and slides out, slow, takes off his sunglasses.

                    DELIVERYMAN
Jesus Christ, man, don't shoot me!

                    SOMERSET
Turn around. Hands on your head!

                    DELIVERYMAN
What the hell's going on?

                    SOMERSET
Who are you? What are you doing out here?

                    DELIVERYMAN
I'm . . . I'm just delivering a package.

INT. POLICE HELICOPTER – EARLY EVENING

California listens as the chopper spins over industrial parks.

                    DELIVERYMAN
                 (voice-over; through headset)
It's just a package for this guy . . . David. Detective David Mills.

                    CALIFORNIA
Motherfucker.

The Pilot looks back at California.

                    PILOT
Let's do it.

                    CALIFORNIA
No! Wait for Somerset!

EXT. MARSHLANDS – EARLY EVENING

Mills and Doe can see Somerset keeping his distance from the

Deliveryman. The Deliveryman moves to the back of the van and opens the van's rear door.

JOHN DOE

When I said I admired you . . . I meant what I said. I do admire you.

Mills keeps his eyes on the van, but steps up to place his gun at the back of Doe's head. Pulls the hammer back.

MILLS

Shut up.

EXT. MARSHLANDS. INDUSTRIAL ROAD – EARLY EVENING

Somerset comes to put his gun right behind the Deliveryman's ear.

SOMERSET

Slowly.

The Deliveryman nods, reaching to take a brown package, about a foot square, from the van.

DELIVERYMAN

This . . . this guy paid me five hundred bucks to bring it out here. He wanted it here at exactly seven o'clock.

SOMERSET

Put it down. Put it on the ground.

DELIVERYMAN

Okay . . .

He puts it on the road and backs away, holding up his hands.

Somerset glances into the field to see Doe on his knees with Mills behind him. Somerset looks at the package. Written on top: DETECTIVE DAVID MILLS – HANDLE WITH CARE.

SOMERSET
(*to Deliveryman*)

Face the van. Do it! Face it with your hands behind your head.

Somerset keeps his gun on the Deliveryman and his eye on the box. The Deliveryman presses his face against the side of the van.

Somerset frisks him hastily, shoves his hand in the Deliveryman's back pocket and pulls out his wallet.

SOMERSET

Turn around.

The Deliveryman obeys. He's scared. Somerset goes through the wallet, shaking it, dumping its contents on the ground.

He bends to retrieve the driver's license, looking at it and comparing it to the Deliveryman's face. Somerset pockets the license, then moves to the van, opening the driver's door.

Somerset examines the driver's area, looks under the seat, then takes the keys from the ignition and pockets them. He motions to the Deliveryman.

Climb in . . . get me your registration.

DELIVERYMAN

Alright . . .

Somerset backs up, keeping his gun trained, while the Deliveryman climbs across the front seat. Somerset pulls back his bullet-proof vest and speaks into the mike.

SOMERSET

There's a package here. It's from John Doe.

Somerset doesn't know what to do. He walks around the package.

I don't know . . . I don't know . . .

The Deliveryman warily brings over the registration. Somerset glances at it, shoves it in his pocket, then reaches to take the Deliveryman's ID tag off his uniform.

Somerset looks out towards Doe and Mills, then looks back at the package.

INT. HELICOPTER – EARLY EVENING

California waits, listening, looking into the blood-red sky.

SOMERSET
(*voice-over; through headset*)
I'm going to have to open it.

EXT. MARSHLANDS – EARLY EVENING

Mills watches Somerset push the Deliveryman away.

JOHN DOE
I wish I could have been a normal man like you. I wish I could have had a simple life.

MILLS
What the fuck is going on?!

EXT. MARSHLANDS. INDUSTRIAL ROAD – EARLY EVENING

Somerset shoves the Deliveryman away.

SOMERSET
Go. Run!

The Deliveryman gladly starts running down the industrial road, not looking back.

Somerset turns. He walks, kneels in front of the package, reholstering his gun, talking into his microphone.

I sent the delivery guy out on foot . . . back towards the city. Call it in . . . have him picked up. He's heading east.

Somerset pulls his switchblade, clicks it open.

I'm opening the package now.

He cuts across the top of the box, hands shaking, cuts quickly.

He fumbles with the thick tape, ripping it.

He pulls the box open, pulls at some bubble-wrap inside.

INT. POLICE HELICOPTER – EARLY EVENING

The Pilot grits his teeth.

PILOT
(*into helmet mike*)

Let's go!

CALIFORNIA

We are going to wait!

California listens.

SOMERSET
(*voice-over; through headset*)
Oh, Christ . . . Oh Christ . . .

EXT. MARSHLANDS. INDUSTRIAL ROAD – EARLY EVENING

Somerset stumbles backwards, away from the open box.

He is horribly shaken, eyes filled with numb fear. He leans against the van for support, retches, sick, holds the back of his hand to his mouth.

SOMERSET

No . . .

EXT. MARSHLANDS – EARLY EVENING

Mills is watching Somerset; he grabs John Doe by the shirt.

MILLS

Get up. Stand up! Let's go!

Doe stands, tries to walk. Mills is moving quickly, towards Somerset. Doe can't keep up.

JOHN DOE

You've made a good life for yourself . . .

MILLS

Shut up!

Doe falls and Mills starts dragging him through the weeds.

EXT. MARSHLANDS. INDUSTRIAL ROAD – EARLY EVENING

Somerset wipes saliva from his lips and tears from his eyes. He takes a deep breath, looks to see Mills dragging Doe.

SOMERSET

Oh, fuck, no . . .

Somerset straightens, tries to pull himself together. He swallows, draws his gun.

>   (into hidden mike)
> Listen . . . listen to me. Whatever you do . . . don't come in here. Stay away. No matter what you hear, do not move in!
>   (starts towards Mills)
> John Doe has the upper hand.

Somerset picks up his switchblade and flips the blade back in. He enters the marsh.

EXT. MARSHLANDS – EARLY EVENING

Mills sees Somerset coming and pulls Doe so that Doe stands.

>   JOHN DOE
>   (quietly, watching)
> Here he comes.

>   MILLS
>   (shouts to Somerset)
> What the fuck is going on?

>   JOHN DOE
>   (to Mills)
> I want you to know, I wish I could have lived like you do.

Somerset starts running towards Mills, mud splattering.

>   SOMERSET
> Mills . . . put down your gun! Throw it away!

Mills leaves Doe behind, walks towards Somerset, gun down.

>   MILLS
> What?

Somerset is fifty yards away and closing.

>   SOMERSET
> Throw your gun down now!

MILLS

What are you talking about? What happened?

JOHN DOE

Are you listening to me, Detective Mills? I'm trying to tell
you how much I admire you . . . and your pretty wife Tracy.

Mills freezes, turns to Doe. Doe smiles. Somerset is close.

SOMERSET

Throw your weapon, detective! Now!

MILLS
(*to John Doe*)

What did you say?

JOHN DOE

It's surprising how easily a member of the press can purchase
information from the men in your precinct.

SOMERSET

David . . . please . . .

JOHN DOE

I visited your home this morning, after you left.

Mills is filled with aching terror.

I tried to play husband . . . tried to taste the life of a simple
man, but it didn't work out. So, I took a souvenir.

*Mills turns to look at Somerset with pleading eyes. Somerset holds out
his hand.*

SOMERSET

Give me the gun.

JOHN DOE

Her pretty head.

MILLS

Somerset . . .

JOHN DOE

Because I envy your normal life. It seems envy is my sin.

143

Somerset can't hold back tears.

Fury rises in Mills and he turns to level his gun at John Doe.

Somerset raises his gun and points it at Mills.

SOMERSET

No!

Mills sees Somerset's gun, raises his gun to Somerset.

MILLS

Tell me it's not true.

SOMERSET

I can't let you do this . . .

Mills steps forward, enraged.

MILLS

Put your gun down!!

SOMERSET

Don't do this . . . please . . .

MILLS

Put the gun down, Somerset!

A pause. Somerset's gun hand is trembling. The wind whips across them. The HELICOPTER can be HEARD distantly. Somerset throws his gun down.

SOMERSET

David, listen to me . . .

Mills goes to grab John Doe by the throat and puts the gun to Doe's forehead, blind with rage.

Somerset holds his hand behind his back, opens his switchblade.

He wants this! He wants you to do it!

Doe is staring into Mills' eyes with wild expectation.

JOHN DOE

Kill me.

Doe lowers his head, waiting for execution.

Mills holds the gun at Doe's head, undecided, furious.

Somerset edges towards them.

> MILLS
> *(looks to Somerset)*
> Stop it! You stay away!

Somerset moves the switchblade so he's holding it by the blade, ready to throw, keeping it hidden.

> SOMERSET
> I can't let you do this!

Mills kicks Doe and throws him backwards on the ground. The HELICOPTER is CLOSER.

Mills stands over Doe and points the gun.

> JOHN DOE
> She begged for her life, and for the life of your baby inside her.

Mills' face fills with confusion – then a wave of horror.

Doe's eyes register shock.

> You didn't know.

> SOMERSET
> NO!

Somerset brings his hand out to throw the blade, but Mills reacts to the movement, turns on Somerset and fires – BLAM!

Somerset flies backwards in the air, the bullet exploding into his shoulder, just above the bullet-proof vest's opening.

Somerset hits the ground, crying out, bloody, writhing.

Mills turns the gun on John Doe.

INT. POLICE HELICOPTER – EARLY EVENING

The chopper is over the marshland. California is leaning out with his

rifle. He cringes from the sound as FROM HIS HEADSET is
HEARD: BLAM – BLAM – BLAM – BLAM – BLAM.

INSERT – TITLE CARD: TWO WEEKS LATER

INT. HOSPITAL ROOM – DAY

Somerset sits in a wheelchair. He is dressed in a hospital gown. His
upper chest and shoulder are wrapped in bandages. He stares out the
window at the city's buildings.

                    CAPTAIN
                  (*off-screen*)
        Hey there, Somerset.

Somerset turns to see the Captain. Somerset looks weak, older.

                    SOMERSET
        Hello.

The Captain walks in, carrying something behind his back.

                    CAPTAIN
        How you feeling?

                    SOMERSET
        I can breathe without pain now, so I guess I feel great.

Somerset musters a lame smile. The Captain sits on the bed.

                    CAPTAIN
        The guys at the precinct heard you're getting out today.
        Anyway, we all chipped in . . .

The Captain takes a big tool belt full of tools from behind his back. He
hands it over. Somerset looks at it and lays it on his lap. He smiles for
real.

                    SOMERSET
        Thank you. Tell them, thank you.

                    CAPTAIN
        We figure you need all the tools you can get to fix up that
        piece of shit you call a house.

SOMERSET

Yeah, that's true.

Somerset continues examining the tools.

CAPTAIN

They're hoping you stop and say goodbye before you go, but I told them not to expect it.

SOMERSET
(*not looking up*)

It would be too hard.

The Captain stands.

CAPTAIN

I have to get going, but . . . there is one more thing.

Somerset looks up. The Captain takes a letter from his pocket.

I don't know if you're going to want it. It was down front. It's from Mills.

Somerset pauses, then puts out his hand to take it.

He's being arraigned tomorrow.

SOMERSET

I read about it in the paper.

Somerset just looks at the letter.

CAPTAIN

I guess . . . decide for yourself. I don't know what it says. I'm going to go.

SOMERSET

I'll see you.

The Captain nods, walks into the hall.

Somerset wheels back to the window. He looks at the letter. Pause. He opens it. Unfolds the paper inside.

The note reads:

> YOU WERE RIGHT. YOU WERE
> RIGHT ABOUT EVERYTHING.

Somerset closes the note, upset.

INT. HOSPITAL. MAIN NURSES' STATION – DAY

Somerset is in street clothes. He signs a form at the busy front desk. A NURSE takes the form and hands Somerset a large manila envelope.

                    NURSE
There you go, Mr Somerset.

'Mr' causes Somerset to look strangely at the nurse.

   Yes?

                    SOMERSET
   Nothing.

EXT. HOSPITAL – DAY

Somerset comes down the stairs, slowly, drained. He holds the manila envelope. The streets are busy with pedestrians and traffic.

He walks down the sidewalk.

He stops. He opens the manila envelope to look inside.

He sorts through the contents, takes out his keys and puts them in his pocket.

He reaches in the envelope again, and takes out the square of wallpaper with the pale, red rose on it.

There is some dried, brown blood on the paper. Somerset lays the envelope on the ground at his feet.

He looks at the rose, tries to scratch off the blood.

He looks up, squinting from the sun, at the city bustling around him. At the tight canyon formed by the buildings.

At the cars, buses and taxis racing in the streets.

At a man, talking to himself, who lies on the sidewalk, surrounded by garbage.

At the people, miserable people, walking past him.

Somerset takes out the note from Mills:

> YOU WERE RIGHT. YOU WERE
> RIGHT ABOUT EVERYTHING.

He lets out a sigh.

SOMERSET
(*to himself*)

Oh . . . man . . .

He sighs again, so tired.

He puts the pale paper rose inside the note from Mills.

He folds them together.

He tears them both up, into little pieces.

EXT. OLD HOUSE – DAY

The house from the first scene. The MAN in the real estate broker's jacket crosses the muddy lawn. He's carrying something.

It's a FOR SALE sign. He shoves the sign's pointed tip into the ground, pressing down on it, leaning with his weight against it.

He uses a hammer to pound the FOR SALE sign back in place in front of the old house.

The world is a fine place,
and worth fighting for.

Ernest Hemingway, *For Whom the Bell Tolls*, 1940

Stills from
Seven

Director David Fincher